JOINING THE DOTS

An unauthorised biography of

PRAVIN GORDHAN

JOINING
the
DOTS

An unauthorised biography of
PRAVIN GORDHAN

Jonathan Ancer & Chris Whitfield

JONATHAN BALL PUBLISHERS
Johannesburg • Cape Town • London

© Text Jonathan Ancer and Chris Whitfield 2021
© Published edition 2021 Jonathan Ball Publishers

Originally published in South Africa in 2021 by
JONATHAN BALL PUBLISHERS
A division of Media24 (Pty) Ltd
PO Box 33977
Jeppestown
2043

ISBN 978-1-77619-105-5
ebook ISBN 978-1-77619-106-2

Every effort has been made to trace the copyright holders and to obtain their permission for the use of copyright material. The publishers apologise for any errors or omissions and would be grateful to be notified of any corrections that should be incorporated in future editions of this book.

www.jonathanball.co.za
www.twitter.com/JonathanBallPub
www.facebook.com/JonathanBallPublishers

Cover by publicide
Cover image by Eyewitness News
Photograph of Pravin Gordhan and Jacob Zuma by Gallo
All other photographs provided by Pravin Gordhan
Design and typesetting by Martine Barker
Set in Avenir/Le Monde Livre

Contents

Introduction

Jonathan Ancer

I watched Pravin Gordhan make his way to the podium in parliament to deliver his department's budget speech. It was 11 July 2019 and members of the Economic Freedom Fighters (EFF) were spoiling for a fight with the public enterprises minister.

A year earlier, the EFF had been among Gordhan's most effusive praise singers, but now they heckled him and threatened to stop him speaking – even if they had to use force. Moments later twenty EFF members of parliament in red overalls stormed the podium.

Grace Boroto, who was presiding over the sitting, was concerned they would physically attack the minister. But Gordhan, a grim look on his face, didn't flinch. He stared down the red berets.

I remember being impressed by Gordhan's steely resolve.

I knew Gordhan had been involved in the struggle for freedom, but I didn't know the details about the actual contribution he'd made. Gordhan is a household name, but there isn't a great deal in the public domain about his background.

In July 2020, a year after the EFF's parliamentary bust-up, I got the opportunity to delve into Gordhan's history when fellow journalist Chris Whitfield and I set out to write his unauthorised biography. We asked ourselves what we hoped to achieve with the book. For starters, we wanted to trace where he came from and track his political trajectory. We wanted to know how he came to be the face of the resistance against state capture and whether he really is that exceedingly rare beast: a clean politician.

I was also curious to find out more about Gordhan's steely resolve.

Ultimately, though, we wanted to know what it is that makes Pravin Gordhan tick. We set out to do what Gordhan had told the country to do at the memorial service for struggle icon Ahmed Kathrada in 2017: connect the dots.

To get a grip on the role that Gordhan has played in the country, we interviewed a broad range of people he's interacted with throughout his life: comrades and compatriots, associates and advisers, cabinet ministers and colleagues, communists and economists, friends and … well, okay, we didn't speak to his foes (more about them later).

Speaking to 1970s Natal activists, we learned that when he was in his early 20s Gordhan devoted his life to dismantling apartheid. He and his comrades Yunus Mahomed and Roy Padayachie were a triumvirate that pioneered mass mobilisation in the province, a concept that was rolled out throughout the country. 'The Durban Moment', as it became known, resulted in the resuscitation of internal resistance, which the state had effectively crushed during the 1960s.

Many of those Natal activists put their lives on the line, took enormous risks and made huge sacrifices for South Africa's liberation. They're among the thousands of unsung heroes whose contribution to the anti-apartheid cause has gone largely unacknowledged.

Gordhan worked above ground, was active in the underground,

and also operated in the shadowy world between the two. He was involved in civic organisations, the Natal Indian Congress (NIC), the African National Congress (ANC) and the South African Communist Party (SACP).

It was while trawling through evidence before the Truth and Reconciliation Commission (TRC, which operated from 1996 to 2003 to help deal with what happened under apartheid) that I caught a glimpse of Gordhan's resolve of steel. He had endured beatings and been tortured by the security police, but no matter what his torturers meted out, he refused to cooperate or divulge anything of value to them about another activist. He would rather have died than succumbed.

The more we delved into his history, the more I realised that Gordhan's life is tied to South Africa's struggle for liberation and that he's had a hand in a number of watershed moments, taking on different roles and functions as he faced the demands of each new challenge.

He played a significant role behind the scenes in the formation of the United Democratic Front (UDF), which brought together diverse groups to shake apartheid to its core.

He helped to shepherd South Africa through the fragile Convention for a Democratic South Africa (Codesa) and Multiparty Negotiating Forum (MPNF) process that saw the country shed apartheid and embrace democracy.

He participated in the drafting of South Africa's constitution and spent five years in parliament helping to develop local-government authorities.

As South African Revenue Service (SARS) commissioner, he transformed the revenue service into an efficient and effective tax authority.

His 2009 appointment as the country's finance minister put him on a collision course with the forces of state capture.

The more we looked into Gordhan's life, the more questions we had. We wanted to know at precisely what moment he realised that the state had been captured and how he felt about his former comrades who'd betrayed the principles on which the struggle had been built. How did he feel about becoming the poster child for the resistance and having the responsibility to clean up corruption?

And, of course, I wanted to know where he gets his steely resolve.

We realised that to form a comprehensive picture of Gordhan – to properly connect the dots – we would have to connect with the man himself. But that was easier said than done. We asked people close to Gordhan about the possibility of setting up an interview with him so that we could explain our project and what we hoped to achieve.

The answers came back: 'I'll try, but don't hold your breath …'; 'You know, Pravin is actually very shy …'; 'The minister is a private person …'; 'PG doesn't like talking about himself …'; 'Minister Gordhan loathes talking about himself …'; 'PG dislikes talking about himself …'; 'Pravin hates talking about himself …'

Eventually, after many people had pleaded our case and vouched for us, we managed to achieve where the Guptas had failed: we wore him down. Gordhan agreed to give us an audience.

We logged into the Zoom meeting at the appointed hour and watched as his image came into focus. We explained that we wanted to write about his public life. He nodded. 'Okay,' he said. 'What's your first question?'

'Er, um, well,' we spluttered.

We'd been so busy polishing and rehearsing our arguments appealing for his cooperation that we hadn't prepared any questions.

We arranged a number of interviews over the months. He answered every question we posed. He had facts and figures at his fingertips and recalled extraordinary details from events half a century ago. Gordhan, who's in his 70s, has incredible stamina. After one two-and-a-half-hour session, in which he'd done all the talking, I could barely keep my eyes open.

'You look more tired than me,' he declared.

I was. It was a Sunday evening and, despite having worked the whole day, he still had another meeting to go to.

In our sessions with Gordhan, we never saw him lose his composure or become flustered, but, then again, we never called him arrogant or a racist bully or told him to shut up – as former SARS commissioner Tom Moyane's advocate Dali Mpofu did when he cross-examined him at the Zondo commission.

We didn't speak to Gordhan's foes: the EFF, Jacob Zuma and his 'radical economic transformation' (RET) gang, Iqbal Survé and Piet Rampedi, and the like. We tried. We sent messages asking if we could explore their criticisms in greater depth, and we asked them to share with us the evidence of the accusations they've levelled against Gordhan. They didn't respond, which probably says all you need to know about the substance of their allegations.

When his opponents wouldn't provide us with evidence against Gordhan, we went searching for the dirt ourselves. We couldn't find any. Yes, people talked about how he doesn't brook opposition and can be an exacting micromanager who gets grumpy when he doesn't get his way. Someone even suggested he was a slavedriver, who demanded loyalty, focus and dedication from his staff. (If he'd been our publisher, we may even have met the deadline for this book.)

There were grumbles about his abrasiveness but there wasn't a single hint of impropriety. 'Incorruptible' is how most colleagues described him. They spoke about his integrity and described him as principled, moral and thoroughly scrupulous.

So is Gordhan, in fact, that exceedingly rare creature, a clean politician?

My guess is that he would be the first person to shake his head – not because he doesn't see himself as clean, but because he doesn't consider himself a politician. He sees himself as a community worker, an activist.

It's why he joined the freedom struggle and it's how he became a major obstacle in the state-capture project. He drew a line in the sand when Jacob Zuma went nuclear on him after Nenegate in 2015, and tried to dislodge him as the finance minister. He stood up to the attacks launched by the former president and his allies.

For Gordhan, it's always been about 'the higher purpose'. And that, I realised, is the source of his steely resolve.

Chris Whitfield

When we were commissioned to write this book, I put on my figurative hazmat suit and prepared to head into the toxic world of politics. I'd been out of mainstream media for several years and had mostly adopted the jaundiced view of the current crop of commentators: that we're governed ineffectually and there's very little cause for optimism.

My co-author, Jonathan Ancer, and I dipped our toes into the project by interviewing old comrades of Pravin Gordhan from the 1970s and 1980s. We soon realised we were dealing with an extraordinary set of people: brave, thoughtful, decent and wise.

Some of them are in the later years of their lives and a few of their contemporaries have died. This is itself a cause for sadness, but more so because so many of them are unsung heroes. Yes, heroes: their commitment to this country and their selflessness have been heroic. They wouldn't ask for it, but their courage and valour deserve greater recognition.

We also turned to former work colleagues of Gordhan for their impressions. In this process it became evident that the public sector had lost people of the very highest calibre during the presidency of Jacob Zuma. One example: the contribution that Ivan Pillay could have made to governance if he hadn't been hounded out of SARS is probably immeasurable. There is, of course, a personal element to this: Pillay's career was cut short in a brutal fashion and he's suffered financially as a consequence. But we South Africans have also been robbed of the contribution of a thoughtful person who could have continued helping heal a country still wounded by its past.

Pillay wasn't alone in being purged, and this led us to another realisation: that the damage inflicted during the Zuma years runs far deeper than its breathtaking financial losses. SARS, for example, has been denied the qualities of the likes of Pillay and others, but also much more: the successful culture of a 'higher purpose' that Gordhan and his lieutenants had instilled in the service was diluted and then destroyed. The systems they'd developed to make the tax collector a world-class department were also weakened or broken.

Many other government entities were similarly stripped of talent, culture and systems. We were told of a number of accomplished and important civil servants from various government departments who headed into the private sector when they realised just what was going to be required of them under the Zuma administration. These people were the cream of the crop – the ones who could comfortably find work elsewhere.

The culture of service that earlier presidents and ministers in the post-apartheid era had been trying to build was dashed before it really got going.

But we also met people working in the current administration who had somehow weathered the Zuma storm and have since rolled up their sleeves and got on with the job of rebuilding the country.

Many of them are also remarkable – committed and smart.

Good people have also been brought back into service by the Ramaphosa administration.

And then there's Gordhan himself. There's a lot of smoke around him and we expected to find some fire, but we didn't. Instead, we found somebody who's devoted his entire life to the service of this country and whose primary motivation seems to be simply to make it a better place for all of us.

Of course, he's flawed – who isn't? – but whatever his faults may be, they don't appear to have interfered with that objective, and it's surely one we should treasure in our public leadership.

The commentariat – the journalists and broadcasters who analyse and comment on current affairs – isn't much given to praise or optimism these days. Heaven knows why, but journalism is increasingly coming to seem like the social-media space that has done it so much damage.

But this journey and the people I've mentioned gave me, at least, hope.

Prologue

The wheels had just touched the tarmac at Heathrow Airport early on that Monday morning in 2017 when Finance Minister Pravin Gordhan – often called 'PG' by those close to him – switched on his cellphone. The South African economy was underperforming and he was at the start of a pre-arranged high-profile roadshow to the United Kingdom and the United States to promote the country as an investment destination.

As the aircraft taxied from the runway to the terminal, his phone pinged. There was a message from Cassius Lubisi, the director-general in the presidency, whose job it was to carry communications between the president and the various heads of government departments.

What now? Gordhan thought, as he opened the message.

To: Honourable Minister Pravin Gordhan,
Honourable Deputy Minister Mcebisi Jonas,
Director-General Lungisa Fuzile
From: Cassius Lubisi,
Director-General in the Presidency
Date: 26 March 2017, 22h13

Good evening, Honourable Minister and Honourable
Deputy Minister.

By order of His Excellency the President, I have been
directed to communicate an urgent message to your good
selves, that the permission for you to travel to the UK and
the USA from 26 to 31 March 2017 has been rescinded
with immediate effect. In that regard, His Excellency has
directed that I request that your good selves return to
the Republic of South Africa as soon as you receive this
message. Further, His Excellency has directed that you
instruct [Director-General] Lungisa Fuzile to accompany
your good selves back home. His Excellency the President
will be dispatching a formal directive to your respective
offices tomorrow morning, 27 March 2017.

Gordhan disembarked into a crisp spring London morning,
wondering what this sudden recall was all about. Since his reappointment as finance minister fifteen months earlier, he'd been under
attack from all quarters. He'd been set upon by the crime-busting
unit the Hawks – the country's Directorate for Priority Crime
Investigation, set up by Jacob Zuma's administration in 2008, which
targeted organised and economic crime and corruption – and the
National Prosecuting Authority (NPA), which had thrown spurious
corruption charges at him.

The relentless pressure was taking a toll on his health, but at
this stage, almost a decade into the presidency of 'His Excellency',
Gordhan had no illusions about the sheer depth and width of the
corruption that was tearing the country to pieces, and he was determined to fight it. It was no secret that he was engaged in political
warfare with President Jacob Zuma, his former struggle comrade

with whom he shared a birthday, and the man at the centre of the state-capture project.

Gordhan spotted Lungisa Fuzile and showed him the message. The two men stood in the airport, considering what to do. When the president instructs you to return immediately, you do so, but there was no immediate flight from London. They decided to continue with the meetings for that day, including two with global ratings agencies, and a teleconference call with a third ratings agency.

It was 6am and the delegation had been flying for twelve hours. Gordhan made his way to a hotel, showered, changed, bolted down some breakfast and took a call from his deputy, Mcebisi Jonas, who was to head up the second leg of the investor roadshow, to the United States, and was at that stage still in South Africa. He'd also received the text message and wanted to know what was going on.

'I don't know,' Gordhan told him.

'Maybe he's going to fire us now,' said Jonas.

'Maybe,' Gordhan responded. 'We'll see.'

By 8.30am Gordhan was in his first meeting.

A little more than 24 hours after Gordhan had touched down in London and read the text message ordering him to return home, the wheels of the plane bringing him back to South Africa raised smoke on the tarmac at Johannesburg's OR Tambo International Airport, delivering the finance minister into a political firestorm.

1

The Making of an Activist

He's heavy, thought Abba Omar, when he first met Pravin Gordhan in the late 1970s – a description of the then long-haired, bearded firebrand similar to those of others who knew him at the time. Serious, determined and focused, Gordhan was described as 'bookish' and 'very serious' by some peers.

Yacoob Abba Omar served the ANC in various capacities prior to South Africa's first democratic elections in 1994, and the ANC government in various capacities after those elections, including as the country's ambassador to Oman and then the United Arab Emirates. But back in the 1970s, he'd just made his way to the University of Durban-Westville and was drifting into student politics. At the time, Gordhan – idealistic, and determined to change the world – had already left university, and was operating in legal political activity, quasi-legal political activity and completely illegal political activity in the underground.

Gordhan's reputation as a committed activist had spread into Durban's Indian neighbourhoods, where the memory of the apartheid government's iron-fist crackdown of the 1960s was still fresh and had produced a cowed community who lived in fear of getting on the wrong side of the security police. Most people steered clear of politics and avoided activists.

But for Gordhan, says Omar, 'Activism was, like, 99.99 percent of Pravin's life.'

Pravin Gordhan may now be 72, clean-shaven and bald, but he's still imbued with the fiery commitment of the activism of his youth. 'We've come some way in the last 26 years, and among the younger generation there's some level of cohesion taking place, but at the same time the fractures of the past remain with us,' he says on 16 December – the country's official Day of Reconciliation. The date is also the anniversary of the launch of the ANC's armed wing, Umkhonto we Sizwe (MK), and on this day in 2020 Gordhan is reflecting on what it means to him. He says it's about remembering the sacrifices activists made in the liberation struggle, and it's about continuing to get good South Africans to contibute towards social cohesion and nationhood. 'It's a reminder of the kind of heart but also the vision and the maturity and the farsightedness of the leadership that [Nelson] Mandela, [Walter] Sisulu and others represented,' he says. 'That's what reconciliation is about, notwithstanding our differences.'

Pravin Jamnadas Gordhan was born in Durban on 12 April 1949, a year after the apartheid government came to power. His parents were immigrants trying to carve a new life for themselves. Jamnadas Gordhan and his wife Rumbaben were from the western part of the Indian state of Gujarat, not too far from the Port of Porbandar, where Gandhi was born.

The first Indians had come to South Africa in the 1860s as indentured labourers and worked on the sugar plantations in what was then Natal. Jamnadas, however, had been born into a family of jewellers, known as Sonis, and the Gordhans were part of the so-called passenger Indians: traders with small business skills who were commercially oriented and were seeking opportunities abroad, and who entered the country under the ordinary immigration laws, and at their own expense.

They settled in Durban in the 1920s and lived in a fairly rundown building in Bond Street in the city centre, which was popularly known as the Grey Street area or Durban's casbah. It was a working-class community of Muslim, Hindu and Christian families, seen as Durban's equivalent of Johannesburg's Sophiatown or Cape Town's District Six. The young Gordhan found the mix of religious backgrounds fascinating and grew up in an environment where a Muslim person referred to a Hindu person as his sister or brother, and whether you were Hindu or Muslim or Christian didn't matter.

His childhood wasn't exceptional for a boy in his community in the South Africa of the day: he was born in a country in which he couldn't sit on benches marked for Europeans only; when he went to parks, he had to watch with his arms folded while other children played on the swings – swings he couldn't touch because they were reserved for white kids. He learned to play cricket and soccer in the street, not on a sports field, because there wasn't one in his neighbourhood, not even at the school.

In the mid-1950s Gordhan senior started to import saris, and opened his own store in the Grey Street area. Gordhan junior worked in the shop on weekends and during school holidays but being in business didn't appeal to him.

Durban's Indian population was growing and there was a demand for special saris from India for significant events like weddings. In a space of a few years, Jamnadas Gordhan had opened three shops. All was going well until someone let him down financially and he went insolvent. The Gordhan family went through a particularly tough period in the 1960s.

While the young man was aware that there were places he couldn't go because of the colour of his skin, he figured that was just the way life was. His parents weren't political ('I was the black sheep,' he says with a wry grin). It was only when he went to Sastri College, an Indian boys' high school, and a couple of teachers drifted away from their subjects and talked to the boys about philosophy, literature and a version of history that wasn't through the lens of the National Party (NP) that Gordhan's eyes began to gradually open and he started to realise that racism was an issue.

His advance down the road of full-blooded activism took a great leap forward in 1968 when he registered to study pharmacy at Durban's University College for Indians (which would in 1972 become the University of Durban-Westville, and finally, post-apartheid, one of the campuses of the University of KwaZulu-Natal). The campus was based at the former navy barracks on Salisbury Island in the Port of Durban, and the students travelled by ferry from the mainland to the island.

The deputy registrar, a white Afrikaans man, met the ferry at the island each morning. He wasn't there to welcome the students, but to inspect them as they disembarked. He checked the length of their hair and made sure they were wearing a tie. If the students failed his inspection, he put them back on the ferry and sent them home.

Durban's air was heavy with humidity during the sweltering summers, and on one particularly unpleasant day the students in Gordhan's stuffy chemistry class took off their ties. It was just too hot. Their lecturer told them to put their ties back on or he wouldn't teach. The students walked out.

On the surface, their departure may not have seemed political, but it was very much an act of defiance against the university's authority – an authority strongly aligned with apartheid.

Almost the entire university administration was made up of white Afrikaners, and it was known to be led by Broederbonders, exclusively male, Calvinist members of an Afrikaner 'brotherhood' dedicated to the advancement of Afrikaner interests. The influence of the Broederbond, founded in 1918, was strongest during the rise of apartheid, which was largely designed and implemented by members. Many prominent figures of South African political life, including all leaders of the government, were Broederbonders.

At the University College for Indians, some of the administrators were rumoured to have links with the dreaded Security Branch security police, known for the torture, extralegal detention and forced disappearance and assassination of anti-apartheid activists.

Gordhan was searching for a political home during this time, and had a range of experiences that led him further and further along the path of activism. He attended events at the Phoenix settlement, an area about 25 kilometres northwest of Durban, founded by Gandhi in 1904 and established as a township by the apartheid government in 1976, but with roots as a sugarcane estate and a long history of Indian settlement. These events were organised by activists in the NIC, founded by Mahatma Gandhi in 1894 to fight discrimination against Indians in South Africa. Many of the activists were banned and placed under house arrest. Banning, a form of 'internal exile', was a repressive measure used by the South African apartheid regime and entailed restrictions on where the banned person could live and who they could have contact with, and forbade them from travelling outside a specific magisterial district. They couldn't attend meetings of any kind or engage in any political activity, with the penalty for any violations up to five years in prison.

Gordhan went to the Durban City Hall to listen to the Progressive Party, which at the time believed in a qualified franchise.

Considered the left wing of the then all-white parliament (represented for many years by a single member, Helen Suzman), the party opposed the ruling NP's policies of apartheid.

Gordhan read the works of German-American philosopher, sociologist and political theorist Herbert Marcuse, and French philosopher, author and journalist Albert Camus. He pondered the pros and cons of Trotsky's 'permanent revolution', in which a revolutionary class pursues its own interests independently and without compromise or alliance with opposing sections of society. And he took an interest in the emerging grassroots activist Black Consciousness Movement; although he never became an adherent of its philosophy, it raised his awareness.

Gordhan also became involved in campus issues, and was voted onto the 1971/1972 student representative council (SRC). As far as the university's management was concerned, however, an independent student council was out of the question, and the administration would only allow the SRC to function on its terms. The SRC submitted a constitution to the administration, which was returned with the words 'with the prior approval of the rector' after everything they wanted to do, such as publish a newsletter, invite guest speakers and produce press statements.

As an example of the administration's interference, Gordhan recalls the students wanting to invite a speaker as part of the orientation of the first years in 1972. Curiously enough, the person they had in mind was Mangosuthu Buthelezi, then a member of the ANC Youth League, and chief executive officer of the newly formed Zulu Territorial Authority, a region intended by the apartheid government as a homeland for the Zulu people, but the administration refused, arguing that Buthelezi was too liberal.

The SRC called a mass meeting to protest against the administration. Students gathered in a large lecture theatre but before the meeting could begin, the university's fearsome six-foot-plus regis-trar – and one of the university officials believed to have security-police ties – came in and told the students they couldn't meet in the lecture theatre because it was a fire hazard, and ordered them to vacate.

The students regrouped in the canteen, where they resolved to hold a two-day boycott and suspend the SRC until they could have a student government body that was acceptable to them. This decision became known as the '72 Resolution. The upshot was that the SRC remained in abeyance for the rest of the decade.

The university administration ran an annual orientation pro-gramme for first-year students, to put out a strong propaganda line about how to be a good student and obey the rules. After the SRC was dissolved, Gordhan and his fellow activists launched their own orientation initiatives off campus to conscientise first-year students. They recruited students into adult-education programmes and com-munity projects in working-class areas, and held cultural events in town. In addition, they hosted sessions at Phoenix settlement that they called Farcity, consisting of skits critiquing the university's administration and highlighting the wrongs of South African society in general.

Students recited their own poems, the political poetry of German Marxist Bertolt Brecht, and verses from a range of African and Russian poets. They also performed the witches' scene from *Macbeth*, portraying some of the university's administration as the witches brewing a plot to keep everybody in subjugation.

They put on a version of *Sizwe Banzi is Dead*, a hugely popu-lar and highly charged political drama by Athol Fugard, John Kani and Winston Ntshona. The students renamed the play *Sizwe Banzi is Alive* because they wanted it to have a positive message about students taking control of their own lives. Gordhan was involved in the production but no one can remember clearly if he acted in it – not even Gordhan himself. 'I doubt it,' he ventures.

Then ANC activist Ivan Pillay was in the audience, and believes Gordhan had a part in the play and thinks he may have even been sporting a ponytail. Yousuf Vawda, today a lecturer at the University of KwaZulu-Natal School of Law, but a student at the time, suspects Gordhan was more behind the scenes because 'he's the least skilled in terms of singing or acting and he'll be the first to admit it'.

⬦

That year – 1972 – proved to be a formidable period in student politics. It was driven largely by the Black Consciousness Movement protesting against what was essentially apartheid tertiary education.

The dissent began in May, when Abram Tiro was expelled from Turfloop campus (now the University of Limpopo) for criticising the university's graduation ceremony, for which white people packed the audience while black parents, whose children were actually graduating, were shut out.

Tiro was a prominent member of the South African Student Organisation (SASO), which had been formed in 1968 after some members of the University of Natal's Black Campus SRC decided to break away from the National Union of South African Students, a liberal organisation dominated by white students. Students on black campuses across the country, including Durban-Westville, embarked on two-week long lecture boycotts to protest against Tiro's expulsion.

Yousuf Vawda remembers the police descending on the Westville campus during the protests. 'Seeing the full might of the law on campus was highly politicising for all of us,' he says.

Gordhan, who was very much in the core of the campus

leadership, was moved by the student solidarity across the country and inspired by the power of protest. He'd been reading about strategy, tactics and principles of struggle, and the boycotts provided an opportunity to put the theory into practice.

Most political books were banned and he consumed any scraps of literature he could get his hands on, like essays from Vietnamese communist politician Lê Duân, who was the general secretary of the Vietnamese Communist Party, and anti-apartheid campaigner Mary Benson's prohibited 1962 book *The African Patriots: The Story of the African National Congress of South Africa*. Gordhan listened to the ANC's Radio Freedom, a crime that carried an eight-year jail term. Every year on 8 January, the anniversary of the ANC's founding, he would tune in to hear Oliver Tambo's annual message to see where the movement was heading.

⟡

When Gordhan had first walked – or sailed – onto the Salisbury Island campus in 1968 he wasn't an activist, but when he graduated from the Westville campus in 1973 he had a strong affiliation to Congress politics and was a committed activist.

There wasn't a watershed moment that led Pravin Gordhan to become an activist. His journey to activism was incremental, and encompassed experiences of injustice; dealing with the university's verkrampte administration, which opposed any changes toward liberal trends in government policy, especially relating to racial questions; being exposed to the Freedom Charter – the 1955 statement of core principles of the South African Congress Alliance, which included the ANC and the South African Indian Congress (SAIC) – and getting to know members of the NIC, and becoming familiar with its history and principles. His university years proved to be a period of pulling all the political pieces together and developing his political consciousness.

The moment he knew he'd become a full-blown activist, however, was when Durban's University College for Indians moved to West-ville, and the university administration invited the vicious apartheid prime minister BJ Vorster to open the shiny new campus. On the morning of Vorster's address, a group of students blitzed the campus with thousands of bright-yellow stickers bearing the slogan 'Vorster Go Home'.

The students boycotted the prime minister's speech and arranged an anti-Vorster rally at a nearby hall. While Gordhan waited for the crowds to take their seats, a burly Security Branch policeman marched up to him and glared at him. This particular security police-man had a reputation for being brutal and provoked fear in all he confronted. Gordhan, however, stood his ground.

Fifty years later, he's still doing the same thing.

2

The Making of a Philosophy

The Umgeni River slices through the northern parts of Durban, its normally sluggish brown waters spilling into the sea at the Blue Lagoon. But it's not always placid.

According to Neelan Govender and Viroshen Chetty in their 2014 book *Legends of the Tide: Roots of the Durban Fishing Industry*, when the Umgeni River is in flood it's 'as large as a python and as fast as a viper' and swallows everything: 'dogs and chickens, carts and carriages, goat sheds and goats too'. In 1917 torrential rains caused the river to burst its banks and 'wave after wave, the Umgeni dumped its dinner of shredded trees, corrugated iron sheets and carcasses'.

Tin Town, a shack community on the Springfield Flats near the Blue Lagoon, was submerged in those floods. The community was made up of over 2 500 people who'd turned the riverbanks into lush vegetable gardens, and hawked their produce door to door around Durban. They'd experienced flooding many times over the years but this was the worst. Residents were swept away in the waves, battling the current. Some managed to climb onto the roofs of their collapsing homes, pleading to be saved, but police abandoned their rescue attempts, fearing for their own safety.

Mariemuthoo Padavatan, a seine-netter, and five other fisher-men made five trips into the raging river in an oar-driven boat. The Padavatan Six, as they became known, saved 176 people from drowning and their rescue effort is considered one of the country's most impressive civilian acts of bravery.

More than four hundred people lost their lives in the floods and almost all the farmers lost their livelihoods. The Tin Town residents picked themselves up and rebuilt their shantytown settlement, replanting their vegetables.

In March 1976 the Umgeni misbehaved again and heavy rains flattened Tin Town once more, leaving thousands of residents, who had had very little to start with, with nothing. Former member of an MK cell in the Durban Central area and later Robben Island prisoner Sunny Singh recalls visiting the community after the floods and sinking into mud. 'The floods swept all those veggie gardens and the homes away. People were absolutely destitute,' he recalls.

In a strange twist, the deluge was pivotal to the development of the strategy of mass mobilisation and made a significant contribution to dislodging the apartheid government.

By the time of the 1976 Tin Town floods, 27-year-old Pravin Gordhan had graduated from university and was working as a pharmacist at King Edward VIII Hospital in the Durban suburb of Umbilo – but that was mostly just cover. His real job was on the political front, where he was exceedingly busy.

He was on the executive committee of the newly revived NIC, which at the time was functioning mostly as a committee, but its influence could be felt and its affiliation to the Freedom Charter seen. Gordhan, who'd been recruited into the ANC, had been making contact with the first wave of political prisoners who'd served their sentences and were coming off Robben Island – activists like Sunny Singh, Jacob Zuma and Mandla Judson Kuzwayo. He was also part of an informal activist collective, along with microbiologist and re-search chemist Roy Padayachie, medical physicist Goolam Aboobaker, attorney Yunus Mahomed, and Yousuf Vawda. The five comrades met regularly to develop a finer understanding of politics. They discussed what was happening on campus, and studied Marxist literature and the works of leaders of the African liberation movements.

But, notes Vawda, they realised that they weren't doing enough. 'Of course, we wanted to change the world, so we felt that we needed to do a little more, because reading groups were not going to bring about fundamental change.'

The five set up classes for African students at Emmanuel Cathe-dral in Durban. Giving classes to African students was illegal unless you belonged to a 'cultural club' registered with the government. So they established a club and got their students to join. They organised poetry readings and protest theatre in the community.

But they felt that that still wasn't enough.

When Frelimo, the nationalist movement fighting for the inde-pendence of the Portuguese 'overseas province' of Mozambique, won its struggle in 1975, SASO and the Black People's Convention (an umbrella organisation of the Black Consciousness Movement with origins in mainly white, liberal universities) held a series of pro-Frelimo rallies across the country. The rally at Curries Fountain stadium in Durban is still vivid in Gordhan's memory.

The authorities banned the demonstration under the 1956 Riotous Assemblies Act, which prohibited gatherings in open-air public places if the minister of justice considered they could endan-ger the public order, and the police set their dogs on the protesters. Gordhan wasn't a good athlete and struggled to make it across the field before the sharp teeth of the law could sink into his flesh.

The police arrested the SASO leaders and a seventeen-month trial of the so-called SASO Nine followed. All nine were convicted and sentenced to between five and ten years on Robben Island.

In the wake of the Frelimo-rally crackdown, many activists felt the only way to continue with the liberation struggle was to go underground, but Gordhan had a different view. He wasn't convinced that these protests were particularly fruitful, because although they were important symbolically, they didn't lead to organisation. His thinking at that time was about recruiting activists and building up organised groups.

Goolam Aboobaker says they discussed the possibility of venturing into the trade-union movement, 'but somehow we thought, as Indian activists, our main challenge was to organise working-class communities, Indian working-class communities'.

Since their student days, the activists had been grappling with the Marxian concept that it's the masses who make history, and a key question they wrestled with, and kept returning to, was: How do we organise the broader community? 'In other words,' explains Gordhan, 'how do you connect to the people? How do you get into mass mobilisation? And that led to the idea that, given the political conditions and constraints that we worked under, we needed to get involved in community issues.'

The 1976 Tin Town floods presented the group with an opportunity to give meaning and life to the concept of community mobilisation. 'We cut our teeth on dealing with communities in working with Tin Town,' says Aboobaker. People were reluctant to engage with politics after the crackdowns of the 1960s and by the time of the Tin Town floods the security forces were enforcing apartheid with impunity. However, a doctor who would be resistant to standing up and declaring his allegiance to the ANC publicly, would happily run a clinic, and this turned out to be a useful way to conscientise people.

It was a period of the gestation of a strategy that was internally focused, not just reliant on the armed struggle and going into exile, which had become the inevitable route for activists, but using local issues – urgent and immediate problems – to develop community-based organisations.

Some of the Tin Town residents who'd had to vacate their homes after the floods remained in the area in temporary tents, while others were placed in emergency shelters in Asherville, a few kilometres away. The activists were worried that the people still living in the waterlogged area would contract waterborne diseases like cholera. 'Some of our colleagues were at the medical school,' says Gordhan, 'and they'd developed a health screening programme.' They also ran a clinic to treat residents.

In what Vawda describes as their 'big break', the activists initially got involved as volunteers doing social relief work, like raising funds and getting groceries to help the people in that desperate situation. 'But then, through the contacts we made in those communities, we started to understand the need to form committees. We formed a local residents' association and a crisis committee to help work with those people to articulate clear demands in the [Durban City] Council.'

Those demands for proper housing and basic services, which the neglected Tin Town community had been denied for decades, became a rallying call and a way to draw people into the national struggle.

According to former ANC intelligence operative Moe Shaik, what was absolutely critical to the success of that mobilisation strategy was to keep overt politics out of it. In other words, recruiting activists in that repressive climate was a political sleight of hand. 'Fundamentally,' he explains, 'you're organising people in order to raise their consciousness to challenge the state, but you don't say that upfront. You don't say, "We're coming together to overthrow apartheid," because then you would have lost everybody. So you say, "We're coming here to organise ourselves to get better housing, and we can't get better housing because the Durban City Council has a racist approach to us, and therefore we need to win little victories against the Council." We were taking up issues in the community, and Pravin was very central to that.'

The University of Durban-Westville was a rich ground to recruit students to join the relief work. The volunteers and the community members were invited to participate in classes where they received a crash course in Marxist concepts like historical materialism (which argues that history is the result of material conditions rather than ideals), and learned about the history of the ANC and the Congress movement.

Vawda says the people who came through these ranks would make the connection between their own suffering and the apartheid Pretoria administration – and although the Gordhan comrades were careful not to openly push political messages, they were able to recruit people into the political engine of the NIC, and later into the ANC, and eventually into the underground structures.

When Ivan Pillay, who'd arranged a prefab office in which the Tin Town community could keep food supplies because everything was just full of water, visited Tin Town, he noticed that Gordhan's group had earned the respect and confidence of the people because of their involvement in their day-to-day struggles.

What was key about the Tin Town mobilisation, says Aboobaker, was the adoption of the M-Plan, a strategy of organising ANC members into small cells in each street, which had been devised by (and named for) Nelson Mandela in the late 1950s. The M-Plan had been drafted to ensure the ANC could continue to operate underground in the event of its being banned. The ANC had indeed been declared illegal in 1960 but unfortunately the state's onslaught on the organisation and its leadership meant the M-Plan hadn't had much success.

Dusting off the M-Plan to implement it in Durban two decades later was a collaborative effort, and many activists were involved in the Tin Town mass mobilisation, but many of the community activists at the time agree that it was Gordhan who spearheaded this strategy.

'Pravin was a very formidable organiser,' says Aboobaker.

'Pravin was the master of mobilisation,' says Shaik.

'Pravin understood mass orientation and was able to drive organisation,' says Vawda.

'Pravin pioneered OCMS,' says Vidhu Vedalankar, an activist from the time, referring to 'organisation, consciousness, mobilisation and struggle', 'the idea that communities had to be mobilised around issues that impacted their everyday life, and to link that understanding of the everyday realities to the bigger reality.'

That 'bigger reality' was, of course, apartheid.

◈

For Yousuf Vawda, the mobilisation was the start of a very meaningful way of interacting with the community. He explains, 'One of the things the Tin Town experience taught us was how important it was to work with local communities, and how, by connecting with local problems, one could develop a whole range of things, relationships, organisations and campaigns, which enabled people to take control of their lives, and not have somebody else do things for them.'

A cohort of local leaders emerged out of these initiatives, and the activists trained them how to negotiate and take up their issues with the Durban City Council.

After a year-long struggle, the demand for alternative housing was won and residents were relocated to Phoenix. The Council divided Phoenix into precincts or units, and began to build low-cost housing there for the Tin Town refugees. However, the Council didn't provide many schools or other community facilities, so children had to travel to and from Clare Estate, thirty kilometres away.

Gordhan's group followed the Tin Town residents to Phoenix township. 'There were two units in Phoenix, one called Stonebridge and one called Clayfield. Clayfield became our playground,' Gordhan says.

Big meetings were prohibited, but there were no facilities where people could gather anyway, so the activists went door to door and arranged house meetings. Vawda says, 'We would invite all the households in that street and about thirty people would come. We would talk about their issues and problems, and how they needed to be taken up, and usually that culminated in calling for volunteers and ultimately setting up committees that would take up the campaign.'

That, says Gordhan, is how the Clayfield Residents Association started. 'By 1978 we'd brought several of these associations together and created the Phoenix Working Committee. That became quite militant, because we started confronting the education authorities for schools, and the municipal authorities for sports fields and clinics. We started linking Natal Indian Congress activity with this community activity, and slowly merged the two. Some leaders in the NIC were willing to now stick their necks out, and come out into community meetings and mass meetings and mass protests, and that just grew.'

The community organised major campaigns against high rentals, and embarked on rent boycotts. It was painstaking work and happened over a long period of time, and they didn't always have success, but there were visible victories. When the next Phoenix unit was established, a sports ground and a school were built along with the houses.

Another success story saw apartheid take a body blow. In the 1950s the government came up with the concept of 'New Towns'. In what was the government's homeland policy on a local level, these towns were to be created as self-contained municipalities with their own rates base and their own facilities, and would be cut off from the white municipalities. Two towns were earmarked as pilots for this project: Mitchells Plain in Cape Town and Durban's Phoenix, which was billed as 'the Indian City of the Future'.

By 1978, with a few units of Phoenix developed, the government decided to put its New Town plan into place and excise Phoenix from Durban. Resistance from the Phoenix residents prompted the then Natal provincial authority to establish a commission to investigate whether the community should be separated from Durban.

An intensive campaign to mobilise the community against the New Town concept was launched. When members of the commission inspected the area, they were met by furious residents holding placards demanding that Phoenix remain part of the city. 'The Security Branch watched the protesters but those people weren't afraid,' recalls Gordhan. 'The protests gathered momentum, and a year and a half later, the commission reported that it was not viable to separate Phoenix from the city of Durban. It was a massive victory.'

The mobilisation strategy also gave Gordhan access to an informal network, and in that way helped him carry out ANC missions.

⊹

Meanwhile, Gordhan had been holding secret meetings in dark corners of the King Edward VIII Hospital with ANC activist Mac

Maharaj, who'd been convicted in 1964 on charges of sabotage and had served a dozen years in prison, and had just come off Robben Island. Maharaj was aware of Gordhan's work at the community level and how his group had become involved in mobilising the Tin Town community.

'I was very impressed,' says Maharaj, 'not only with the work Pravin's group was doing but with the thinking and reading that they were putting into it. They were familiarising themselves with literature, as much as they could find from around the world, on how to organise. And we found ourselves, him and I, very much on the same wavelength.'

Similarly, NIC veteran Thumba Pillay developed an admiration for Gordhan and the crop of activists under his wing. 'They weren't just talkers and theorists, but doers in the real sense of the word. They were out there among the people, taking up issues that affected their everyday lives. They were active in establishing ratepayer organisations, housing action committees, flood relief, slum clearance, education action and a host of community-based organisations [working to alleviate the burden of] those suffering under the yoke of apartheid.'

Aboobaker says that it was Gordhan who brought together all these various civic organisations and residents' associations.

That Tin Town model of using people's grievances to mobilise them began to cross over into different Indian areas, such as Chatsworth and Tongaat, and into adjoining African townships like Lamontville, Hambanati and Chesterville, and then linked up with the coloured areas. 'By 1980 we had a non-racial movement going,' says Gordhan.

Mpho Scott, then a leader of the Congress of South African Students (Cosas) from Lamontville, recalls working with Gordhan on a powerful ongoing campaign against rent increases called Asinimali (which means 'we don't have money'). 'Pravin is a born strategist,' he says. 'He could look at a problem and immediately see what it was that was needed and what it was that could be done. During that period there was a lot of emphasis on political education.'

Indeed, the political-education component was key. For Gordhan, the strategy worked not because of the mobilisation but because of the way people were mobilised. It was the instilling of a particular purpose and planting the right kind of political consciousness that led to sustained organisation. That purpose, he says, provided the value system and the political principles – such as non-racialism and non-sexism – on which to base the organisation.

✦

In the then Transvaal, Ismail 'Momo' Momoniat and Mohammed Valli Moosa both matriculated in 1974. They were politically conscious and were strong supporters of the Black Consciousness Movement. Momoniat went to the University of the Witwatersrand (Wits) in Johannesburg and Moosa enrolled at the University of Durban-Westville.

In the 1970s, black students studying at historically white universities established 'black students' societies', elected bodies representing the specific interests of black students, and Wits was no exception. Momoniat, who became involved in the Wits Black Students Society and embraced Black Consciousness philosophy, says, 'After the June Soweto Uprising, I began to feel that Black Consciousness wasn't taking us anywhere. We were, I guess, more angry, and anger against the enemy itself wasn't going to get us freedom. We felt that the problem with Black Consciousness was that it was almost stuck in student politics.'

In the meantime, Moosa had met Gordhan and Yunus Mahomed

in Natal, and he had shared their approach of mass-based politics with Momoniat.

'We started arranging meetings in the community,' says Momoniat. 'We learned from what Pravin and Yunus Mahomed were doing, and we went on door-to-door visits. We organised street committees in Lenasia, Laudium and Benoni, and we started working in Soweto with activists like Amos Masondo and Popo [Molefe].' Masondo had established underground MK cells in Soweto, and Molefe was a founding member of the Azanian People's Organisation in 1978.

'Activists looked to the work that was being done in communities in Natal and they rolled that out in the townships in Transvaal and in other parts of the country,' Momoniat continues. 'Pravin inspired that.'

One of these activists was the Soweto-based Mandla Nkomfe, a member of Cosas and the Soweto Civic Association, which was formed in 1979. 'We were interested in building organisations, getting involved in resistance, and taking up campaigns around the cost of living and against the black local authorities,' says Nkomfe. The Black Local Authorities Act of 1982 provided for the establishment of a series of local government structures similar to those operating in the South African apartheid 'white' areas; councillors elected by local residents were responsible for township administration on budgets raised by local rents and levies. These local authorities were highly controversial and seen as puppets of the government.

Nkomfe made contact with groups in Cape Town, Port Elizabeth and East London, and in Natal. 'We learned the most about organisational work in Natal, and in particular through PG and the people he was working with. He guided us on issues, taught us how to run an organisation, how to go to people's houses, how to distribute pamphlets, and how to analyse your own problems and find solutions. PG was very useful to us in the early 1980s.'

Nkomfe says that the Soweto students were eager to learn and wanted to absorb as much as possible, and Gordhan became their mentor. 'Here was a person who understood the science of organisation, and who was very strategic and could simplify complex concepts.'

Former Robben Islanders taught the students about the politics of the ANC, and Gordhan explained to them the objectives of the organisation and taught them how to reach out to ordinary people and mobilise them, says Nkomfe. 'He gave us a lot of confidence that we can do these things, and we went back to Soweto to organise, and to pull together people's grievances to raise their consciousness to confront authority. He taught us that what we were doing was about service to the people ... It was about changing the world. It wasn't about ourselves.'

❖

A range of formations flowed out of the Tin Town experience: the Durban Housing Action Committee, which was a conglomeration of local civic groups; the Action Committee to Stop Evictions, which campaigned against the Group Areas Act; the Joint Rent Action Committee to oppose rent increases in Durban townships; the Soweto Crisis Committee, which was established to combat the appalling Bantu Education system; the Durban Women's Group, set up to ensure women's issues were an integral part of the struggles being waged; and the Cape Areas Housing Action Committee.

Sandy Africa, a Durban-based activist at the time, says it's because of Gordhan that a generation of citizens and activists could see the value of community engagement and were able to effect change. 'I think he instilled those ideas of the theory of change, which involves mobilising people into organisations that put pressure on authorities. He inspired them to question their values and reshape the way in which they see the world. That's one of his lasting legacies.'

This intense period of mobilising communities, raising political consciousness and activating activists was, in essence, the resuscitation of the liberation movement's internal resistance, which the state had smashed in 1963 when the police had rounded up MK's High Command at Liliesleaf Farm and put ten of them on trial to face charges of 193 counts of sabotage against the state, resulting in life sentences for eight.

When the Umgeni River burst its banks in 1917, the Padavatan Six came to the rescue of Tin Town and the Durban City Council gave them gold medals for their bravery. When the Umgeni flooded six decades later, the Gordhan Five – Padayachie, Aboobaker, Mahomed, Vawda and PG – mobilised activists and inspired the community to take charge of their lives and confront the Durban City Council. It's no surprise that the Council didn't reward Gordhan and Co with gold medals.

3

The Politics of Non-Participation

When Durban lawyer and firebrand political activist Thumba Pillay's banning order finally expired in 1975, he made his way to a clandestine meeting of the NIC executive. Pillay had heard a great deal about Pravin Gordhan and the other up-and-coming leaders who'd gained recognition for their militancy and activism, but it was at that secret NIC meeting that he interacted with Gordhan for the first time.

Pillay was impressed with Gordhan's political discipline and his calm, sober and rational approach to issues. He was immediately drawn to PG, whom he found to be 'not just a learned student of struggle history steeped in theory only, but a doer, one who would get down on his hands and knees and get things done, never one to stand aloof from rank and file'.

Four years later and on a different continent, Pillay and Gordhan attended another secret meeting. This time, they were on the opposite ends of a fierce ideological debate. The people attending this highly classified meeting in London had been chosen carefully and with circumspection from a security point of view, to resolve a contentious dispute raging among Indian activists in Durban:

should they participate in the South African Indian Council elections or not?

The South African Indian Council was a government advisory body set up in 1964 to make recommendations about matters affecting the Indian community. Made up of nominees by the minister in charge of Indian affairs, it was seen as a toothless government stooge. When the apartheid state announced in 1979 that it wanted to hold an election for the Indian community to choose 40 of 45 representatives to the South African Indian Council, a bitter debate about what to do nearly tore the NIC apart.

As NIC and ANC stalwart Ismail Meer points out in his 2002 memoir *A Fortunate Man*, activists were of one mind in rejecting any separate institution, but differed sharply about the tactics that should be employed.

The issue refused to go away and reached Mac Maharaj, who was then the secretary of the ANC underground.

Soon after Maharaj had been released from Robben Island in late 1976, Gordhan had gone to seek political counsel from Maharaj, whom he regarded as a legend. Gordhan knew that he had a sharp intellect and a good strategic approach, and he had a long history in the movement which his group of young activists could benefit from. Maharaj became his mentor.

Now was the time for the mentor to intervene.

'There were comrades arguing that because of the conditions imposed by illegality, it was necessary to consider using the state machineries – to go in them, and from within, mobilise both against the state and mobilise for the struggle,' explains Maharaj. 'There were the others who were saying these institutions are tainted and we must not be part of them. We must boycott them, finish and klaar.'

Maharaj encouraged discussions, but for him the litmus test was which approach would 'maximise the unity of our people in action' –

that would 'get out of theory and into the issues of practice'.

The non-collaboration debate, as Maharaj points out, has a long history in the country's liberation movement. 'It was there in the [1936] Native Representative Council [which consisted of six white officials, and four nominated and twelve elected Africans], where the ANC participated and then pulled out. It was there in the Western Cape [in the 1940s], promoted mainly by the [Non-European] Unity Movement circles, [who argued] that there should be no collaboration whatsoever with the state.' Maharaj adds, 'They were not able to implement it in practice, because if you accepted non-collaboration as a principle, then you shouldn't be even working as a teacher or as a government doctor, and you shouldn't be a nurse in government hospitals, and you shouldn't be in the police force, because those were institutions ... that were maintaining the system.'

Maharaj met with Dr Monty Naicker, the banned NIC leader, whose view was that the elections should be boycotted in toto.

Gordhan was in the group that put forward the concept of a 'rejectionist participation': he wanted to participate in the elections with the aim of taking control of the Council, subverting it, and destroying it from within.

Pillay, who was in favour of the boycott, saw in the rejectionist-participation approach an opportunity for the unscrupulous to use the system, ostensibly to make it unworkable but, once in it, to exploit it and live off all the perks it provided, conveniently putting on the back burner the original intention to undermine the system from within.

However, Maharaj believed that Gordhan's group had a formidable argument. 'They were not arguing from the position of armchairs, but as people working at the grassroots, organising and mobilising people on the ground,' he says.

For Gordhan, it was a question of drawing a distinction between principles and tactics. The principle was destroying apartheid, replacing it with a democracy and introducing the Freedom Charter as a programme. The tactic was to use the South African Indian Council as a platform to mobilise various sections of the community against the Council, which was a proxy for the apartheid government.

Reflecting on the debate today, Gordhan explains that although he was part of the Congress movement, his group were making their strategy and tactics up as they went along. 'Nobody told us how to do these things. It was our own development. We were, if you like, political entrepreneurs. We made mistakes and learned and moved on.'

The group had been grappling with the question of how to operate in the oppressive environment. 'We'd read about how Lenin operated within the Duma – let's call it an enemy structure.' (The Gosudarstvennaya Duma, or state assembly, was part of the imperial Russian legislature from 1906 until its dissolution in 1917.) 'He utilised that structure to give him political space to do the things he needed to do. We asked ourselves: Instead of allowing reactionaries to participate in the Coloured Representative Council and later the [South African] Indian Council, why don't we compete for those seats and test the apartheid state as to what latitude we will be given to then use that as a platform to organise and mobilise people? So that, of course, gave rise to intense debate. Some people were virulently opposed to it, and there were others, like us amateurs, who were saying, "Don't shout us down on principle. Tell us about your options."'

Gordhan's group believed that destroying apartheid would happen by activists being on the ground and mobilising people, not by arguing about principles in a committee meeting.

It was around this time that students at the University of Durban-Westville started to reconsider their own boycott of the SRC. A few weeks after they took the decision to resuscitate the dormant

SRC, student activist Alf Karrim approached his fellow comrade Abba Omar and said, 'Well, what do you think about participating in the South African Indian Council as well?'

Omar was taken aback. 'What?' he shot back.

The students had crossed a boundary by participating in the SRC, and now there was talk about them participating in the South African Indian Council.

The students started having their own discussions around the Council elections. 'We had talks among ourselves as students,' says Omar. 'We met with Pravin and with other leadership people like [NIC vice-president] MJ Naidoo, who was quite clear that we should not have anything to do with the Council. Pravin wanted to consider it. His position came from the experience during and after the Tin Town floods and their negotiations with the Durban City Council and the need to go into structures to deliver some kind of relief or structural changes for people.'

Omar recalls that it was an intense debate in the community that literally pitted father against son. 'I remained on the fence,' he says, but adds that many of the activists were convinced by Gordhan's arguments. 'Jay [Jayendra Naidoo, the son of MJ Naidoo] was actually prepared to go against his father's views on the matter. There were more open debates and we hosted a discussion. MJ was invited by some other grouping, and we decided to stand up and walk out while he was talking because we'd agreed to oppose his views. It was a difficult position for young Jay to take.'

The boycott-versus-rejectionist-participation debate raged on and, with the two groups at loggerheads, the ANC asked the members of the opposing camps to attend a meeting in London to resolve the impasse.

Thumba Pillay can't recall how he came to be summoned to attend the talks, and says he arrived in London with no idea whatsoever of the agenda or who would be involved. Pillay was joined in the total-boycott camp by Ismael Meer, whose presence at the talks was fortuitous because he happened to be on a visit to London at the time.

Gordhan had also been summoned to the meeting, where he and Roy Padayachie, who was studying in London at the time, represented the rejectionist-participation camp.

Maharaj recalls devoting a week of full-day discussions with Gordhan and Padayachie. 'We didn't just talk about [the South African Indian Council elections], but how to organise what we were doing, looking at problems, strategy, tactics. I approached the matter with the view that the issue was a matter of tactics, not a matter of principle.'

Maharaj had also been speaking to the other group, and the series of deliberations culminated in a meeting with Meer, Pillay, Padayachie and Gordhan, chaired by the fiercely respected senior ANC and SACP leader Dr Yusuf Dadoo. Activists Frene Ginwala and Aziz Pahad, who were in exile in London, were also at the meeting.

Says Maharaj, 'For the first time, these four people from home were put in the same room, and we discussed the matter, specifically boycott or rejectionist participation. I took the meeting through the issues and explained that it couldn't be a matter of principle, it was a matter of organisation, and which one would under the prevailing conditions be best to organise the masses.'

After two intense days it was eventually agreed that taking the rejectionist-participation route would likely divide the NIC. The group settled on the total-boycott approach and agreed to speak with one voice.

'History tells us that the total-boycott tactic was the correct approach, successfully mobilising the Indian community to unequivocally reject the fraud that it was,' says Pillay.

Maharaj wrote a letter that he and Dadoo signed, stating that they believed the way forward was to boycott the Council elections but added that the final decision should be taken by the activists themselves. 'Nobody knows what happened to that note,' says Maharaj, 'but it effectively brought about unity.'

When Gordhan returned from London and was back at King Edward VIII Hospital, he received a phone call from Yusuf Dadoo. 'So, are we okay?' the eminent ANC leader asked Gordhan. 'Is this matter settled?'

Gordhan told him it was. 'We backed off,' recalls Gordhan, describing the thinking around the rejectionist-participation position as 'a thought experiment'.

Gordhan's group threw its weight behind the boycott effort, and he and Pillay were both elected onto the NIC executive. Reflecting on that meeting more than four decades later, Maharaj says, 'Pravin, like many of us, is stubborn and sometimes I can be annoyingly stubborn, but he is definitely not beyond a rational sit-down discussion. I'm talking about Pravin as a person. When you're strategising, when you're planning, and you're sitting down and debating and you put facts on the table, with all his stubbornness, he's [prepared] to change his mind if you have a case to argue.'

Maharaj says that Gordhan took part vigorously in debates, and that meetings with him were not 'tame'. These debates were a crucial part of Gordhan's life experience, he says, 'because that is a cauldron in which he developed his personality and his steadfastness'.

❖

Gordhan not only accepted the boycott position, he led the campaign to snub the South African Indian Council elections on behalf of the NIC. After a successful 'test run' pulling off a sizable boycott of the

Durban Local Affairs Committee elections in 1979, Gordhan set his sights on the Council election, which the government had scheduled for 4 November 1981.

'We took the 1979 experience one step further and built up an active campaign,' says Gordhan, who was the chief organiser in Durban. Activists were sent to as many places as possible to encourage people not to vote. Rallies were held in Durban, Cape Town and Johannesburg, where the Transvaal Anti-South African Indian Council Committee had been established.

'Pravin was brilliant, frankly,' says Momoniat, who was heavily involved in the Transvaal Anti-South African Indian Council Committee. 'He understood how to open the political space so that we could exploit it. You see, the government wanted credibility for the Council elections, so it couldn't blatantly stamp out the opposition, which meant we could go from town to town to campaign against it.'

There was an ANC flavour to the anti-Council rallies, which were addressed by senior members of the banned organisation, such as Albertina Sisulu, Archie Gumede and Helen Joseph. The campaign took the form of non-racial events where copies of the Freedom Charter were circulated. In fact, in his essay 'Culture and communication: The rise of the left-wing press in South Africa', the author Don Pinnock says the Anti-South African Indian Council campaign launched the Freedom Charter and all that it represented.

In October, more than a hundred organisations attended a meeting in Natal, which the student newspaper *Saspu National* described as an almost unprecedented gathering of progressive organisations.

The words of the Freedom Charter were stuck on the walls at an anti-Council rally held at the Athlone civic centre in Cape Town just days before the election. At that rally, wrote Pinnock, speakers reminded people of the traditions of resistance born out of the Congress Alliance, and about the need for unity and the necessity to boycott undemocratic state institutions.

Goolam Aboobaker was there, and remembers a large ANC flag being flown. The swelling of the anti-Council sentiment pointed to the emergence of a broadly Charterist movement across the country, and that activists and organisations were gravitating towards the ANC.

The boycott of the South African Indian Council election was significant: around ninety percent of registered voters stayed away from the polls, and a little more than one percent of voters cast a ballot in the Johannesburg suburb of Fordsburg.

Despite the Indian community having given the apartheid government a bloody nose, then prime minister PW Botha pushed doggedly ahead with plans to 'reform' apartheid by, in 1983, introducing the tricameral parliament, which would give representation to coloured and Indian South Africans to deal with their 'own affairs' in separate houses. Black South Africans were to be left out in the cold – not that there was much warmth in the Indian and coloured chambers. The NP's three chambers gave the pretence of power sharing, but not only did it banish black South Africans to ten tribal homelands far away from economic opportunities, it continued to vest political power in white hands.

The tricameral parliament was part of a legislative package of constitutional proposals which included three bills by Piet Koornhof, the minister of co-operation and development, who was essentially in charge of 'black affairs'. Two were passed – the Black Local Authorities Act and the Black Communities Development Act – but not the third, the Orderly Movement and Settlement of Black Persons Bill.

These proposals aimed at granting more local-council power to urban blacks while simultaneously tightening influx control, keeping black people trapped in poverty in the bantustans. The Koornhof bills and the tricameral parliament were being sold as a new deal but they were nothing more than putting lipstick on apartheid.

◈

A wave of grassroots activism swept South Africa through the late 1970s and the early 1980s, with a revival of political activity through the Black Consciousness Movement, the NIC and the Soweto Uprising, as well as community-based mobilisation. The resistance took the form of stayaways, marches, pickets, demonstrations, mass rallies, and a range of boycotts – school boycotts, bus boycotts and consumer boycotts of Fatti's & Moni's and Wilson-Rowntree in support of fired workers.

In the midst of this tide of anger, the Dutch Reformed Church cleric and outspoken critic of the NP Allan Boesak addressed the conference of the Transvaal Anti-South African Indian Council Committee on 23 January 1983. 'We cannot accept a new deal which makes apartheid work even better,' he said. 'We cannot accept a future for our people when we have no say in it. And we cannot accept a "solution" which says yes to homelands, the Group Areas Act, to laws which make us believe that we're separate and unequal ... There's no reason why the churches, civic associations, trade unions, student organisations and sport bodies should not unite.'

It was these words that finally led to the birth of an organisation that took apartheid by the scruff of its neck and shook it to its core – the United Democratic Front (UDF).

The momentum had been building for months. Community-based organisations were being formed across the country in the early 1980s and they were beginning to find each other, says Gordhan. 'You had Trevor Manuel and others doing similar work in the Western Cape; you had youth congresses popping up in the

Eastern Cape and Western Cape. Each community was struggling in its own right, each community threw up activists in their own right, each community had a rich Congress presence – either ex-Robben Islanders or people who were banned and then unbanned, or people's families who'd been left behind while they went into exile and the connections still remained ... and that's what eventually gave life to the UDF as a concept,' he says.

Boesak's call was one of a number of independent initiatives that resulted in the formation of the UDF. Two weeks earlier, ANC president Oliver Tambo had raised the idea in his annual 8 January address, saying, 'We must organise the people into strong mass democratic organisations; we must organise all revolutionaries into the underground formation of the ANC; we must organise all combatants into units of Umkhonto we Sizwe; we must organise all democratic forces into one front for national liberation.'

There had also been discussions among Durban anti-apartheid activists about the possibility of cooperating with each other, and these talks had begun to give some shape to an arrangement between organisations to collectively try something.

According to Momoniat, the idea of a national democratic front came from Gordhan and Yunus Mahomed. He says the purpose of this united front was to consolidate mass mobilisation, support the ANC's internal campaigns, and create some coherence around the different types of struggles that were taking place, and also to create an internal, non-racial, political leadership – and to do all of this in a climate of repression. 'It was going to be a mammoth task.'

Over the next seven months, UDF coalitions began to take shape and a working group that included Albertina Sisulu, community activist Mewa Ramgobin and MK member and former Robben Island prisoner Steve Tshwete decided to formally launch this national front on 20 August 1983. On that day delegates representing 565

47

organisations from all over the country gathered in Mitchells Plain with a common purpose: to find creative ways to oppose the apartheid government wherever, whenever and however they could.

This national gelling of organisations with aligned interests resulted in a burst of energy and an intensification of internal resistance. 'The idea took off amazingly, beyond our wildest expectations,' says Momoniat.

The UDF's first fight was against the tricameral elections and the Koornhof bills, which was the basis for a non-racial campaign.

Gordhan, who was regarded as the key architect of the NIC's anti-election strategy, set to work to mobilise communities against the tricameral parliament. It was a highly organised campaign with hundreds of anti-election activists – many of them recruited from Durban campuses – and they gave the campaign person power and imbued it with a festive atmosphere.

The campaign's 'shock troops' worked night in and night out. 'We had maps of every area, and activists took responsibility for a street and made sure they visited every single house to persuade the residents not to vote,' says Gordhan. 'Every weekend similar planning took place, street by street, block by block, throughout the province, visiting house by house to sell the idea as to why not to vote for the tricam, and we began to push the Freedom Charter a little bit during that process as well.'

Pamphlets, leaflets, banners and posters were designed with simple and striking 'Don't Vote' messages. Mass meetings attracting up to ten thousand people were held.

In addition to door-to-door campaigns, the activists used 'letters to the editor' as a way to distribute their message, says Abba Omar, who was also part of the anti-tricameral campaign. Omar drafted the letters and got people to submit them in their own names. 'The Indian community in particular is quite a well-read community, and at that point the highest consumption of newspapers was by the Indian community, even more than the white community, in Durban. They would read these letters avidly, so letters to the editor were free advertising space for us.'

Vidhu Vedalankar, another anti-election activist, says the campaign was so successful because it operated like a well-oiled political machine. The activists would go door to door from 6pm, and then meet up at 10pm in different parts of Durban to assess and analyse the responses from the community. 'We would look at the issues that were coming up and how we needed to respond, and Pravin gave us guidance. The campaign talked to a commitment to organising at a grassroots level and building it up neighbourhood by neighbourhood,' she says.

'There was real passion around,' says Gordhan, 'and all of those campaigns were funded internally. Doctors and lawyers on our side would be the ones to go up to a businessman and say, give us a couple of thousand rands. Some of the businessmen hedged their bets, and would give us a little and give [Amichand] Rajbansi a little.'

Rajbansi served in local government structures, and as leader of the National People's Party stood as a candidate for the house of delegates, the Indians-only parliamentary chamber.

Gordhan continues, 'The campaign took the art of mobilising and organising, and the art of propaganda, to completely different levels … Mass campaigns became our speciality, in a sense, in terms of how to organise them, and scientifically put together a plan that could actually work. In less than ten years, from a post-Rivonia situation of fear of the Security Branch and fear of just two words like "Robben Island", we had a very different scene … A very different scene.'

Omar worked with Gordhan and NIC activist and former Robben Islander Billy Nair in an office that served as the anti-tricameral campaign's HQ and got a front row seat to Gordhan's

49

tactical manoeuvring. 'It was just incredible,' says Omar about how Gordhan outplayed the security police on the day of the election, 28 August 1984, a week after the UDF's first anniversary. 'People got to know that office; people would come there for leaflets. And we had a couple of telephone lines so, of course, the security police also knew about the office and were watching us and listening to our calls. On the day of the election, we shifted the office completely to somewhere else – and only certain comrades in each area knew what the telephone number was for that new office. The cops sat outside the old office. It was brilliant.'

Gordhan and co were being fed reports about what was going on from activists on the ground. 'At one point,' says Omar, 'there were gangs in Chatsworth harassing people and pushing people, especially old people, to go vote for Rajbansi. We had an informal self-defence unit, some guys who were involved with the local karate club, who came in and moered these gangs.'

When the votes were tallied, it emerged that only about twenty percent of registered Indian voters had gone to the polls, and a week earlier, just thirty percent of those registered to vote in the house of representatives – the house for the coloured community – had voted. The boycott movement had become a significant political force, and the unambiguous rejection of the tricameral parliament was a massive boost for the UDF.

The success also ushered in a dark period of repression, as the government moved to crush the resistance. But the genius of the UDF was that it was uncrushable.

'The UDF was a shell,' explains Gordhan. 'By cracking the shell, in other words, banning the UDF, you're doing nothing, actually, because you're leaving the substance of the UDF – the six hundred organisations that constitute it – unbroken and so still alive.

'The UDF was an attempt to create an internal movement

that was Congress in essence and to produce a non-racial leadership. We did it in the early 1980s in Durban because that was our commitment to non-racialism – whatever Malema says today.'

4

Providence

'We're going to watch porno movies' might not be the sort of excuse you would expect an underground operative to use, but South Africa in the late 1970s and early 1980s was anything but normal.

The ruling NP was enthusiastically applying both its apartheid jackboot and an uncompromising moral fervour. Hardline nationalist PW Botha had taken over from John Vorster as prime minister in October 1978, with the latter becoming state president until he was forced to resign a year later over the information scandal – an operation to use taxpayers' money to fund a newspaper, *The Citizen*, that favoured the government.

Television had been introduced to the country in 1976 after years of being regarded as 'the devil's work', but it was aimed squarely at the white population and the South African Broadcasting Corporation's news bulletins were little more than a propaganda channel for the ruling NP. Owning a *Playboy* magazine was a crime, with censorship laws forbidding material that depicted any sexual activity, 'lust' and 'licentiousness'. Gambling was strictly outlawed.

Of course, people found ways around some of this. Those with a taste for gambling would, for example, cross the borders into neighbouring countries with casinos. Some of those resorts contained movie houses, where soft-porn movies were shown and where more than a few South Africans were to be found.

Members of Pravin Gordhan's by then well-established activist unit – called the Providence unit for reasons that nobody seems quite sure about today – had other, quite different, reasons to get into Swaziland.

From the mid-1970s, with security-police activity increasing and many comrades rounded up at home and workplaces as much as places of protest, it soon became apparent that the only way to move forward with the struggle was to go underground. The 1982 Internal Security Act gave the state wide powers of control and coercion, including Section 29, which allowed for people to be detained indefinitely and interrogated using extreme methods of torture such as solitary confinement.

The arsenal of apartheid legislation was being aggressively deployed in just about every area of public life – there were the Group Areas Act, the Population Registration Act, the Reservation of Separate Amenities Act, the Bantu Education Act, the Natives Land Act, the Prohibition of Political Interference Act and many, many more. The Prohibition of Mixed Marriages Act forbade marriage between 'Europeans' and 'non-Europeans', while the Immorality Act closed a potential loophole by prohibiting extramarital sex between white people and those of other races.

Most newspaper headlines routinely reflected two related phenomena of the time: bombings inside the country by the ANC's military wing, MK, and retaliatory raids by the South African Defence Force into neighbouring countries.

The ANC set up the Mandla Judson Kuzwayo unit to provide a channel with the structures of exile in Swaziland, to bring comrades out for training and instruction and, conversely, to bring ANC leaders, information, strategy and tactics into apartheid South Africa.

Yousuf Vawda, a prominent member of the Providence unit at the time, recalls, 'We would be in touch with people like Ivan Pillay and Mac Maharaj outside the country and, on the pretext of going to watch porno movies, we would make lots of trips to Swaziland to go and meet with them and exchange information.'

In 1977, sought by the police, Ivan Pillay, together with his brother Joe, and others, had been forced to establish themselves in exile. Mac Maharaj, following instructions from the ANC, had left South Africa in that same year and was deployed by the organisation in Lusaka, Zambia.

Vawda remembers the late 1970s and early 1980s as a time when the unit was heavily involved in political propaganda, and was also refining its strategy of mass mobilisation. 'They were very interested in the work we were doing because the political organisations weren't able to do what we were able to do. So we would have a lot of exchanges and they were very useful for us to get perspective on the forward area, which was sort of a supply station for people being infiltrated into the country.'

Maharaj, by then the secretary of the underground ANC, encouraged the 'forward area machineries' to link up with the Providence unit to further both the 'political underground' and mass mobilisation. Maharaj says he had discussions with Gordhan about using community grievances to mobilise people. Communities should be encouraged to 'direct the protest to the municipality, so that the municipality is forced to implement what is there in the legislation – use that as a basis to get people into action and come out in support of the liberation struggle', says Maharaj.

It was the philosophy that Gordhan and others refined to great effect. 'Providence was a unique unit in the sense that it wasn't a simple "recruit for MK and conduct one or two operations" unit. It was more of a mass work [mass mobilisation], mass propaganda and recruitment structure,' says Gordhan. 'We didn't take too many chances of silly sorts, but at the same time we were involved in legal political work, legal mass work, semi-illegal mass work, and the underground of the ANC. And eventually the underground of the Communist Party as well. So we had many hats, so to speak, that we wore at that time.'

There was 'no membership card that you're given when you join', says Gordhan. 'This was an organic joining, if you like, of the ANC underground because you made a choice: do I want to be part of this or not? If you were too scared, then you stayed away. If you were willing to take the risk, you moved ahead.'

Pillay, based in Swaziland at the time, remembers Providence having 'a vast reach'. 'They would utilise people from time to time who were not necessarily recruited formally into an ANC structure. It was almost like on a "nod nod, wink wink" basis. And there would be many people like that who were travelling – they carried messages, they carried money.'

Pillay points out that this meant that besides the formal structures, the unit had created a formidable informal capability: 'It involved a lot of professionals – lawyers and doctors in the main.'

Besides its overtly political work, the unit did things such as health screening in Tongaat, and civic work in Phoenix, Chatsworth and Pietermaritzburg, and was active on the campus of the University of Durban-Westville. Although Providence had sprung from the so-called Indian areas, it was committed to non-racialism and worked alongside civic organisations in African townships and coloured suburbs.

Vidhu Vedalankar, who came to the group through student activism, remembers that repression in the townships that fell under the Port Natal Administration Board and were being incorporated into KwaZulu was 'horrendous' and more severe than in areas under the Durban City Council. Nevertheless, the group worked alongside and helped township organisations such as the Joint Rent Action Committee. 'We worked together and we supported them from the NGO [non-governmental organisation] side,' she says.

Vedalankar remembers Gordhan's approach to growing the unit and its reach: 'He was committed to building movements from the grassroots – and his group understood that they weren't the experts. And so that's what they instilled in us. As activists, we weren't allowed to go into townships and into communities and act like we had all the answers. We had to listen and learn from people [and their] experiences.'

There was also a strong emphasis on being guided by facts and data. 'We didn't just dream up things. We had to know and understand the context. We worked with experts at the universities, like people who were in the built-environment area. When we were working in civic struggles, we had people who were town planners and archi-tects helping us understand the issues, understand how things work, how cities work,' says Vedalankar. 'But [we] also [understood] that we needed to discuss and debate everything. You could debate and ask anything. Critical thinking was important.'

Members of the unit also attempted to understand issues in the communities by doing community surveys and trying to build organisations there. 'It was much, much harder [to organise] there,' she remembers.

'In addition to the Community Research Unit, they also estab-lished labour NGOs, and raised funds internationally to do NGO work in support of communities. That was also the start of advice offices set up at local level, to help communities to go and get assistance,' says Vedalankar.

✦

Shamim Meer was a student and community activist in Durban in the 1970s. In 1977, when she returned to Durban from a stint in Cape Town, her husband, Bobby Mare, had been banned, along with her mother, Fatima, a prominent anti-apartheid activist who'd been heavily involved in relief efforts in Asherville after the Tin Town floods of the previous year, and her brother, Rashid. 'That's when I started to work with the group – Yunus, Pravin and others. I would have been active with them from about '78 to about '82, four to five years.'

Meer worked as a social worker for Phoenix Child Welfare during the day, returning to the community to work as an activist at night. 'The work we were doing was based in communities but linked to the national struggle,' she says.

The Providence unit also sought to involve women in its projects. 'When I came into Phoenix, to work with Pravin and Yunus, they were very keen that work happened with women,' Meer recalls. 'I was brought in to particularly work with women in the community. Around 1981 we started the Durban Women's Group with the women who were involved in the housing struggle from the different communities. These were largely communities who'd been rendered serviceless by the Durban City Council.

'We started a publication called *Speak*. By then I was working as a researcher ... and my major activism was with *Speak* magazine, which was really geared at a grassroots constituency – women in communities and women in trade unions – attempting to make sure that the issues that affected women's lives, and women themselves, were a more integral part of the struggles that we were engaging at the time.

'The activist group was growing every day because there were a large number of [University of Durban-Westville] students who would join us and we'd go on weekends to Phoenix to work in the community doing door-to-door visits. I was working in Phoenix, but the other communities were Lamontville, Newlands West, Newlands East, Chatsworth – a wide expanse across Durban – and there were also struggles against the Local Affairs Committees.'

The security police were a constant and ominous presence, but Meer laughs when she remembers a particular afternoon when she was driving Gordhan from Overport to Phoenix in her cream-coloured Volkswagen Beetle and they noticed a Toyota Corolla following them. It was the security police.

'And so Pravin said he would take over driving. He drove like a maniac, trying to get them off our tail … and we went down some side streets and back roads. They were giving chase, and we were trying to get away. And we did. We got them off our tail.'

She's sure the policemen would have known they were going to Phoenix anyway, but laughs: 'It was still fun to have this cat-and-mouse chase.'

She recalls the security police coming to meetings where they 'meant to blend in but they never did'. 'Some of the Indian security policemen … were notorious [but] the sense I have is that these guys were not the main torturers. These Indians had a subservient relationship to the white guys.'

❖

The wide range of Providence's activities 'created a milieu in which you could recruit, in which you could conduct political education', says Gordhan.

Along with leaders like Jerry Coovadia – a doctor who trained in India and the UK, then returned to South Africa to work at King Edward VIII Hospital and later at the University of Natal – the unit played a significant role in schooling a generation of politicians.

'Today, if you speak to many activists who are 55 years old and beyond who went through that period, they'll tell you how they learned their politics through those processes,' says Gordhan.

By the mid-1970s the group had linked up with the NIC and made contact with ANC leaders who'd been released from Robben Island. One of those was Jacob Zuma, and Gordhan and others would transport him to Pietermaritzburg for meetings with ANC Midlands leader Harry Gwala. It was the beginning of a relationship between Gordhan and Zuma that would take them from close comrades to a complete breakdown of trust many years later.

During all this Gordhan continued to work as a pharmacist at King Edward VIII Hospital. But his activism had attracted the attention of the security police, and on 27 November 1981 he was detained at CR Swart police station in Durban.

Ten days earlier, ANC veteran and anti-apartheid activist Griffiths Mxenge had been brutally murdered; many years later five policemen confessed to the Truth and Reconciliation Commission (TRC) that they'd killed him using knives and pangas. Providence unit members were preparing a leaflet to advertise the funeral when Gordhan was arrested.

Two weeks later Gordhan was sitting on the bed in his cell at CR Swart when a policeman came in and handed him a letter from the Natal Provincial Administration. 'It was a sunny day, I remember,' says Gordhan. But the contents of the letter were anything but: '[It] basically said that you're fired as a pharmacist because of your lack of performance.'

Almost six months later, on 7 May 1982, he was released but given a banning order and placed under house arrest – he had to stay in his house from 6pm on Fridays to 6am on Mondays, was restricted to the central Durban magisterial district during the week, and couldn't attend any meetings. The banning order was lifted in 1983.

It was also made clear that he would not get his job back at King Edward VIII Hospital. The Natal Provincial Administration said he'd been dismissed for 'low productivity' and 'continued absenteeism' in spite of the fact that these criticisms had never been raised with him during his eight years of employment. The administration denied that it had anything to do with his detention.

Unsurprisingly, this didn't convince his fellow activists, and the October 1982 edition of *Saspu National* reported that 'a campaign demanding the reinstatement of ex-detainee Pravin Gordhan to his job at Durban's King Edward VIII Hospital is rapidly gaining momentum'.

The Natal Health Workers' Association spearheaded the campaign and was joined by the Medical Graduates Association, the Medical Students Representative Council of the University of Natal, the Alternate Medical Association, the NIC, the Diakonia Council of Churches, the Durban Housing Action Committee and others. Among the activities they launched in support of Gordhan were a media campaign, the widespread distribution of pamphlets, a petition and meetings.

'But I never got my job back,' says Gordhan, who had to then find locum work to earn some income. Later, he set up his own pharmacy in the Grey Street area of central Durban. The pharmacy became a meeting place for activists and a safe place for messages to be exchanged. A fellow activist recalls that the pharmacy never made much of a profit because Gordhan would often not charge for medicines.

Yousuf Vawda remembers another setback for the unit: 'We were busted in 1986 when, I think, a courier who'd been turned by the apartheid state led the police to some of us. I and two or three other members of our cell were busted. I was detained in '87 and spent five months in prison as a Section 29 detainee, and then was released without any charges. Nobody was charged. I don't think they really had enough to go on. We were convincing in our denials, of course, so that helped.'

✦

The people associated with the unit still speak warmly of its leadership. When Shamim Meer became involved in Phoenix, Pravin Gordhan and Yunus Mahomed, who were an entity working in tandem, were inspiring as leaders, she recalls. 'We were all fired up,' she says. 'We were all very passionate about our involvement in the struggle against apartheid and for a new socialist dispensation, which is what we imagined would come into being post-apartheid. We shared a passion, a commitment, and we also shared a feeling that we would continue even despite the costs in terms of the security police, who were constantly surveilling the group. We were prepared to court the dangers of the time for what we believed in, and Yunus and Pravin stood out as very steadfast in this resolve, and were inspiring leaders. Pravin was highly disciplined, and very caring.'

Vedalankar says, 'We saw them as leaders, but what we found interesting was that they were approachable. So it wasn't like they were distant and we couldn't interact with them. They were very approachable. They actually were building this movement and so … they were engaging people like us, who were activists, and many others at the community level, to get involved and to begin to get the movement going. They didn't push any agenda, which was nice, because it wasn't like they were trying to force anything down your throat or indoctrinate you.'

She describes Gordhan's contribution from that time as 'building from grassroots to a broad range of coalitions – [from] local to national to the Mass Democratic Movement' (MDM). The MDM was a loose alliance of the UDF and the Congress of South African Trade Unions (Cosatu); sometimes described as the UDF in another guise, its casual structure made it difficult for the apartheid government to ban.

But there were sometimes sharp tensions between comrades. Moe Shaik also ran a unit in the Durban area and had some strong differences with Providence. 'It was a known thing in the ANC underground, both inside the country and in Swaziland and with the exiles, that the Pravin grouping and our grouping were at odds with each other on matters of strategy and tactics,' he says.

The point of view increasingly taking hold in his unit was, he says, 'Ag man, this mass organisation and mass mobilisation will take fucking forever to achieve our liberation. What we need to do is join the armed struggle. What we need to do is get involved in MK and be part of the attack machinery against the state.

'Pravin, on the other hand, had the view that this was not the way we should be going, that the conditions were not yet ready for that. The conditions were not [right] to get involved in military activity ... without laying the basis of receptivity among our communities.

'Of course, one of the central arguments that the Pravin grouping would have about us was that we were adventurous, we were ill-disciplined, we were lazy. We didn't want to actually do the hard door-to-door knocking.'

There were, however, occasions when they did work together.

In 1985 senior ANC member Ebrahim Ebrahim had been spirited into the country but was being sought by the police. Moe Shaik and his brother Yunus had been looking after him, when Moe was detained and interrogated about Ebrahim's whereabouts. Yunus was brutally tortured by security police in pursuit of the same information.

The brothers realised they needed to hand Ebrahim over to another unit before he got caught. They approached Providence, asking them to take over the role of protecting 'a senior ANC leader', but not naming him for fear of a leak. Gordhan recalls, 'We said, right, leave the chap on that particular corner. He will be picked up from there. And that's how Ebrahim was handed over. We stashed him in a safe place for two months, or something like that – worse than a Covid isolation. One of the Providence unit guys who's a doctor today went to London, made logistical arrangements, came back and then eventually we got him out through Swaziland.'

'I must concede, ultimately, that Pravin was right,' Moe Shaik says today. 'Pravin's approach of organising people and raising consciousness was correct because it kept up the momentum by getting more and more people involved in the revolution.'

Shaik came to this understanding through his own intelligence work when he realised the state had infiltrated MK. 'We could objectively measure MK success against police activity. For every successful bomb, or every successful military act, two MK people were getting detained. So, in a sense, it wasn't efficient ... and the whole concept of organising the armed revolution or the armed struggle or the insurrection had to be reconceptualised. And it was reconceptualised in Operation Vula.'

❖

Providence's ten years of being active ended in the late 1980s with Operation Vula, an ambitious ANC project designed to align the strategies of the party's leadership in exile and the struggle movement inside the country.

'There was no such thing as Pravin's group any longer when Vula happened,' says Vawda. 'Many of us then became involved in different parts of the Vula operation. Some of Pravin's group ... went into a sub-unit that was focusing on the SACP, others went into Umkhonto [we Sizwe], others went into the political ANC group, and so on. So [Pravin's] group then morphed into the Vula network, which had a much larger national network.'

Maharaj, Siphiwe Nyanda and Ronnie Kasrils were the senior ANC people sent into the country for Vula, and part of Maharaj's mission became sorting out the tensions between Gordhan's and Shaik's units. 'I knew that these two units, when I came in, were constantly fighting each other,' Maharaj recalls. 'I worked with these two comrades.'

It seems to have done the trick. On one particular night, Gordhan was going to meet and attempt to recruit a member of the security police. 'But we didn't know whether we were walking into a trap because the Security Branch man put out messages that he wanted to meet Pravin, and Pravin was in hiding,' says Maharaj.

They gathered intelligence on the security policeman in question and decided they would go ahead with the meeting.

'But what do we do if it was an ambush? Now, it was part of Moe's job ... that if it was an ambush, we were going to fight it out and save Pravin. And Moe laughed at me when I went through all the plans for D-Day and he said, "What have you done to me?"

'"What do you mean?" I asked.

'"You've made two arch-enemies work together, and today we're there for each other's lives," Moe said.'

5

Captured by the State

By Durban standards, it was a cold day on 12 July 1990, when Pravin Gordhan pulled up outside a block of flats in Brickfield Road in the suburb of Overport. He was there to meet Amnesh Sankar, who, with Gordhan, had been chosen to be part of Operation Vula.

The Brickfield Road flat was being used both as a residence for a colleague who'd entered the country for the operation and as an administration centre.

Gordhan, in short sleeves in spite of the weather, parked his car in the basement and walked up the two flights of stairs to the flat. He put the key in the lock and opened the door.

The next second he was looking down the barrel of a handgun. Pointing it at Gordhan's head was an officer from the notorious Security Branch in Durban.

Operation Vula had been exposed.

❖

There was, of course, intense secrecy around Operation Vula in 1988 when Mac Maharaj and Siphiwe Nyanda were sent into the country on a clandestine mission by the ANC's leadership in exile.

Gordhan himself had been scheduled to pick up Maharaj from the Swaziland border, but there'd been a communication mix-up and Gordhan had gone to the Zimbabwean border. Maharaj got a taxi to Johannesburg and was driven from there to Durban by Ismail Momoniat.

'There was a knock on my house [door], which very few people knew about, and lo and behold, it was Mac,' says Gordhan.

Many of those involved still point to Maharaj when asked to elaborate on the aims of the operation, saying he held his cards close to his chest and drip-fed information only when absolutely necessary – underground operatives at the time worked on a strict need-to-know basis.

This didn't always go down well with his comrades. Billy Nair was a venerated struggle activist with many years of experience who'd been imprisoned for twenty years on Robben Island. He was one of the first people Maharaj looked up after sneaking into the country via Swaziland.

'The first night I was alone with Billy, he suggested we take a drive at about 11 at night, and we drove down to the Durban beach-front,' Maharaj recalls. 'And he drove me past CR Swart [the police station where the Security Branch offices in Durban were located] and the lights were on on the 11th floor. And Billy said, "Now, you see, that's the floor where we get tortured. Now, it's time we bombed this fucking place."

'And I said to him, "We're not doing it."

'So we went back to my hideout, and we had a moerse argument. I couldn't disclose, even to Billy, the nature of my mission. He thought I was there to carry out MK activity, and he was getting furious that I wasn't agreeing.'

As he and Maharaj sipped on whisky, Nair asked, 'What are you doing here if you can't take orders from us?'

'Who the hell are you guys to give me orders?' responded Maharaj.

'Well, we are the UDF,' said Nair.

'Well, you fuck off – you don't give me orders,' Maharaj shouted.

Nair had come to Maharaj's hideout with a cap pulled low over his face and a walking stick. He put on his cap, grabbed the stick and stormed out, 'swearing black and blue', says Maharaj.

Nyanda, who by that time had joined them in the safe house, was, according to Maharaj, shocked at the ferocity of the argument between two senior comrades.

Maharaj was due to leave for Johannesburg the next day at 5am, but decided that he should first set things straight with Nair. 'I wrote a note apologising to Billy: "Put aside this argument, we're in one struggle, blah blah blah."'

Maharaj went to Nyanda's bedroom with the note in a sealed envelope and asked him to give it to Nair – who, at 7 the next morning, was knocking on the door of the safe house, despite not being supposed to visit it during daylight hours.

'Siphiwe gets up, opens the door. Billy doesn't even greet Siphiwe. He marches to my bedroom. And he finds my bed made and I'm gone.'

'Where's this guy? Why is he gone?' Nair asked.

'You know he was heading for Joburg – he left at 5,' responded Nyanda.

'Oh shit,' said Nair. 'I've come to say sorry.'

'He left an envelope here for you.'

Maharaj finishes the story, laughing: 'He [Nair] opens the envelope. He reads it where I'm saying sorry. He says, "I withdraw my sorry … as long as it's clear that he apologised first.'

Now, many years later, Maharaj is obviously more forthcoming about the operation. In essence, he explains, the external leadership of the ANC sent him and Nyanda into the country on a mission to coordinate the various strands of the struggle – both internal and external – but also to correct a bias that had developed towards armed struggle as opposed to mass mobilisation.

'When we set Operation Vula ... we were creating [an ANC] leadership inside the country that would link up with leadership that had grown outside the country ... and make them operate in a combined legal, military, political way. If you read the Walter Sisulu essay, "We Shall Overcome", you'll see he says that merely adopting the armed struggle doesn't make it the dominant form of struggle. It will become dominant over the course of time through action, but you simply do not make it [that] by prescribing it theoretically. But he said mass struggle remains the foundation.'

Maharaj points to notes made by Oliver Tambo during a meeting of the ANC's politico-military strategy commission in Maputo in 1979: 'In his notes he says, "Hey, we've been going about it the wrong way – we've allowed the armed side to move too far ahead. We've got to get back to this mass [mobilisation]. So how do we do it?"'

This debate gave rise to some tensions, including the differences between Moe Shaik's underground unit and Gordhan's over the issue, with the former favouring armed action and the latter emphasising mass mobilisation. This presented Maharaj with the sort of issues he had been sent into the country to resolve.

Shaik recalls: 'Of course, with Mac coming into the country, it presented a new dynamic. And the new dynamic was that you had an ANC leader ... inside the country who could then bring the various underground units together and combine them with all the various arms of the revolution in the context of very effective communication systems.'

Maharaj's intervention in the Durban region – together with input from Nyanda and Nair – would 'fundamentally change the perceived antagonism between Pravin and ourselves', says Shaik.

'Under the new leadership we started to work very, very closely together – so closely that Pravin's brother-in-law … [who] was a computer specialist, [was] offered to our unit in order to help with the analysis, computer analysis and developing algorithms, etcetera, for our database. So that was a big addition. We also took one other member from the Pravin network into our [unit] and we started to work together. I really started to work very closely with Pravin throughout that period until democracy.'

Gordhan says the newfound cooperation between his unit and Shaik's 'saved the necks of some of our guys' during Operation Vula. For example, he recalls a printing unit that had been located in a cottage on the property of a doctor in Chatsworth. Arms and ammunition were also stored in the building. 'Moe tipped us off: "Have you got something in Chatsworth because the cops are waiting inside." One of the three policemen waiting in the cottage was a captain. Five activists were about to head to the cottage to do some printing, but were called back. So five guys' identity and safety were secured as a result of the kind of work that [Shaik] did.'

Maharaj recalls a debate around this incident. 'One view was that they were wanting to ambush us, [so] we could ambush them: "And what a thing to kill a white captain." The other side of the debate? Moe's side: "Ooh, chaps, you do that and you expose my source because the police will ask, "How did we get caught in this ambush? There's somebody inside our ranks."'

Maharaj decided against any ambush. The five activists were spared arrest and the source in the police remained unexposed.

Gordhan says he and Shaik would go out of their way to enlist the help of sympathetic Security Branch officers. 'Moe was the most successful. If the Security Branch guys showed half a chink that they could be approachable, we would exploit that and see what we could extract from them. Sometimes it was a pittance, but ja.'

Another time when Gordhan had cause to be grateful to Shaik involved activist Tees Maistry, whom Maharaj remembers as having 'an aptitude for preparing ignition devices'. Maistry had been storing hardware in a servants' quarters in Reservoir Hills, and Shaik was alerted to the fact that the police had taken photos of him in the area. Thanks to the tip-off, Maistry was warned against returning to the secret stash.

The pictures, however, didn't show Maistry's face clearly, only his full head of hair, and an activist called Bobby Soobrayan – who years later was to become the director-general in the department of basic education – was arrested because he had a similar hairstyle to the man in the photograph. 'And, of course, he knew nothing,' says Gordhan. 'Bobby got a few knocks in the process for a couple of days, but he came out scot-free as well.'

The cooperation between Shaik and Gordhan continued into the negotiation process that gave rise to the 1994 election, when Shaik was assigned to the Convention for a Democratic South Africa (Codesa) talks as an NIC delegate with Gordhan.

Gordhan had been involved in Vula from the get-go. Before Maharaj had come into the country, Providence unit member Yousuf Vawda had been sent to Mauritius to get instructions and guidelines to prepare for the mission. Among the tasks Vawda had been given was to identify a friendly panelbeater who would be able to engineer Mercedes-Benz petrol tanks.

In the years that followed, says Gordhan, 'we had a range of people, largely doctors and so on, who would go to Avis and hire a Mercedes-Benz'. The Mercedes would then be taken to the panelbeater, who would remove the original petrol tank and replace it with a specially customised tank, half of which would be for fuel and the other half engineered to store arms and ammunition in such a way that sniffer dogs wouldn't be able to smell them.

'So that Mercedes-Benz would then cross over into Botswana. We had a whole range of people who did that, and parked [the cars] in a particular place. [The car] would then be taken away, and the petrol tank would be filled with both fuel and the other stuff that needed to come in. It would come back, the car would go back to the panelbeater, the original tank would be replaced, the customised tank would be removed ... and so arms were brought in.'

The car would then be returned to the car-hire company, which remained blissfully unaware that its vehicles were being used to smuggle arms into the country.

One of the drivers of these cars was Dr Ebrahim 'Baker' Aboobaker, who remembers a hiccup in the plan: 'The bloody engine never switched off. It was one of those diesel Mercs, the ones with the huge tanks. But when I stopped at the border I actually couldn't switch off the car engine.' He got lucky, he recalls, because he had a crying child in the back seat 'and I think the border guy was being generous and he just said okay, I could go.'

On occasion Aboobaker delivered messages across the border to ANC operatives in Swaziland and elsewhere. He never knew what was in the messages. They were written on 'very thin paper', folded and sellotaped together, then inserted into toothpaste tubes. 'Those were the missives and we didn't know what was in them. [We were] curious as hell, but we didn't open them.'

Once, Aboobaker and some other operatives were asked to accompany Gordhan on a crossing into Swaziland on foot from the then Transvaal. He was going to meet Ronnie Kasrils, among others. 'That was in the night. We didn't have to cut the fence or anything, we just had to [climb] through the barbed wire,' he recalls. 'It was a pretty hairy experience because it was dark, without any moonlight, and we were walking on uneven terrain. At times the ground would fall away from you. But it was successful in the sense that we met the people we'd planned to meet. And we did that safely, without any kind of hassle [from the authorities].'

Mpho Scott, Gordhan's joint secretary of Vula's greater Durban region, says their responsibilities included coordinating reports from the various structures in what was then Natal, and setting up underground structures with military and political leadership. This required 'getting to know people or identifying people in different areas, getting their names, running security checks, approaching those individuals, meeting with them and inducting them'.

Maharaj describes the nuts-and-bolts work: 'We had to get involved in the mass mobilisation going on. And we had to get in-volved in providing people and attending to the military side of work. But the military side of work was not so much to carry out military operations. In order to create leadership, my view was that we should train people, organise them, train them in rudimentary combat work, train them in practical exercises of sabotage.

'But you were sifting out from that people who should be sent out for officer training. I believed that we could train the ordinary saboteur-combatant to do a level of combat work without having to go out for training. We could do that in the country. But the crucial element in setting up that long-term struggle was to create an officer corps. Pravin was in charge of that process, with myself as the head of it, Siphiwe as the deputy, and the committee was then really run by Pravin and Mpho Scott and Jabu Sithole.'

⬥

Early in July 1990, police arrested MK and Vula operative Charles Ndaba, who'd been using the flat where Gordhan was arrested, and longstanding member of the underground and prominent UDF organiser Mbuso Tshabalala, which signalled the beginning of the apartheid state's crackdown on Vula.

Maharaj says there's been a lot of confusion about how the operation was discovered by the police because of 'speculation on our side and misinformation planted from the other side – from the regime side'. He, however, is 'ninety percent sure' of the sequence of events that led to the series of arrests, including those of himself, Nyanda, Nair and Gordhan.

'One comrade, Charles Ndaba, had come in from outside. He'd been in the MK operations before in the Natal area, and he now came in to reinforce Operation Vula. He was linked to a chap [Tshabalala] who was a very strong organiser in the UDF circles. He'd been a teacher, but was now organising and had been on the run on the South Coast of Natal. We recruited him first into the political section of Vula but then we moved him to begin to work also in the political-military section.

'That weekend ... different people were supposed to be going on different township projects to work. Charles Ndaba and Mbuso Tshabalala seemed to have had a rendezvous somewhere in Greyville near the racecourse, and a Security Branch [member] spotted Charles and arrested him.

'Did they arrest Charles first? Spot him somewhere, arrest him, then torture him and get him to lead them to Mbuso? I don't know. But the two of them were definitely detained. They were extremely brutally tortured.

'Mbuso didn't know my name, but he knew I was in the country. [He] knew I was from outside. Charles didn't know I was in the country but he knew that Ghebuza [Siphiwe Nyanda's nickname] was in the country. So, under torture, they certainly gave the name of Ghebuza and they identified the [ANC safe] house in Kenville. These two comrades, by the way, ended up being taken to the Tugela River [and killed]. It's been admitted in the TRC.'

In 1999 Lieutenant-Colonel Hentie Botha, a notorious Security Branch leader from Durban, confessed at the TRC to the killing on the banks of the river. 'Under the pretence that he was taking toilet paper from his bag, [Lawrence] Wasserman took the bag with the arms and the black bag from the kombi,' said Botha. 'Once in the thick bush where it opens up against the river embankment, Wasserman put his bag down, and while Wasserman, Tshabalala and Ndaba stood at the river embankment and urinated, [Salmon] du Preez and I took the two silenced weapons from the bag. Wasserman made Ndaba and Tshabalala sit on the ground with their faces in the direction of the river. Du Preez and I came from behind and shot them in the back of the head. After they had fallen, each one of them were shot one shot in the temple. I shot Ndaba while Du Preez shot Tshabalala.

'Du Preez and I removed their clothing while Wasserman returned back to the vehicle to collect the concrete poles, the hessian and the wire. ... [Casper] van der Westhuizen went back to the kombi to keep the kombi under observation. Wasserman cut the wire in lengths and Du Preez and I rolled Ndaba in the hessian. After a concrete pole was placed over his chest and legs, the wire was bound round his body, around the hessian, to keep the hessian and the pole in position. Wasserman and I then threw Ndaba's body from the embankment into the river. Wasserman then assisted Du Preez in doing the same with Shabalala's body after which he was also thrown into the river.

'We placed the clothes which were in the black bag into Wasserman's backpack. Branches were broken from the bushes to obliterate the bloodstains. We remained an hour to ensure that the terrain was clear and that the bodies had sunk. We watched the river to ensure that nothing came up again.'

The bodies were never recovered.

Nyanda, Gordhan and several others were arrested on 12 July, five days after Ndaba and Tshabalala had been picked up. (Sankar had arrived at the Brickfield Road flat ahead of Gordhan and had already been arrested by the Security Branch officer inside.) Maharaj says he 'began to detect surveillance' around him on 15 and 16 July while he was in Joburg, and he was arrested on 25 July. Fellow underground operatives Bobby Nair, Dipak Patel, Susan Tshabalala, Raymond Lalla and Catherine Mvelase were also arrested in the Vula crackdown.

Gordhan's first concern after being caught was about material on him that might compromise the operation: a computer disk, or 'stiffy', as they were known then, an electricity bill that might have led police to his own safe house, and other documents. 'It was all in a little black pouch. But this [Security Branch] guy was alone, so I went to the toilet on one occasion, broke the stiffy and got rid of it.'

Shortly afterwards, the Security Branch officer took Gordhan and Sankar into the street and told them to wait in the police van: 'That gave me a further opportunity to get rid of some of the hot stuff that I had on me.'

Gordhan was taken to the CR Swart headquarters of the Security Branch where 'it became evident that these guys were actually rounding up a lot more people'. 'I think we were split into different rooms at the time. So basically we carried on sitting there – they might have given me a sandwich somewhere along the line. I still had some things on me. But they were in no mood to interrogate and search [me], because they were chasing around looking for others, and I managed to again go to the toilet – on the 12th, 13th or the 14th floor – and the window was open so you could throw anything right out of it.'

An officer checking out what Gordhan was doing saw him throwing out some material. Gordhan says, 'I literally told him, "Watch it.

You fucking open your mouth, the ANC is taking over this government, and see what we will do to you." And that was my safety card. Eventually I even got him, in the early hours of the morning, to take a message out for me.'

Gordhan had arranged with his family that he would tell the police he was staying at his sister-in-law's house in Reservoir Hills so as to not have them search and possibly find material at his safe house. 'And there were some clothes and so on left behind there for credibility purposes.'

He was formally detained on a Friday afternoon and gave his address as his sister-in-law's house. 'Much later I learned that no sooner had they got the address than half a dozen of them pitched up with rifles to verify whether that was the truth. And she managed herself extremely well.'

The previous evening, Gordhan's wife Vanitha had gone to see Shaik and told him her husband hadn't come home: something was wrong. Shaik and fellow activist Dipak Patel went to an ANC safe house in Kenville to see if any of their comrades knew what had happened to Gordhan. Shaik parked at the bottom of the house's long driveway while Patel jumped out of the car and headed up the path to the front door. As Shaik got out of the car he saw somebody appear to hug Patel in the doorway – but the arms he'd seen embracing Patel were actually those of a Security Branch policeman pulling him into the house.

'And just as Moe was going to start walking up this path, a cop pops his head out to see if there's anybody else,' says Gordhan. 'And then Moe realises that the whole game is up, gets into his car and he disappears. He got away by the skin of his teeth.'

It was now evident to Gordhan's family and comrades that he'd been detained. Desperate for confirmation of his whereabouts, the family turned to an unlikely source – Morgan Chetty, then a major in the South African Police uniform branch but also a cousin of Gordhan's wife.

'So they tracked [Chetty] down and visited him. Of course, he thought it was a family visit … and the poor innocent soul didn't know what he was letting himself in for.'

The visitors told Chetty that their family member had disappeared and they had phoned every hospital in an attempt to locate him, but with no luck. Could he help them? 'So he phones CR Swart and he gets confirmation: "He's here,"' says Gordhan. 'And that's how they knew that I was in detention. Of course, later on, his superiors gave [Chetty] a hell of a grilling.'

In democratic South Africa, Chetty became a deputy commissioner to Jackie Selebi, then commissioner of the South African Police Service. 'Not that I had anything to do with it,' says Gordhan.

Little more than a day after his arrest, Gordhan was bundled into a car that headed inland on the N3 and towards a brutal encounter with Lieutenant-Colonel Hentie Botha – the man who later confessed to killing Charles Ndaba – which would subsequently be the subject of acrimonious debate at the TRC.

6

Torture

In 1999 Pravin Gordhan, by then the commissioner of the South African Revenue Service (SARS), was shopping with his wife and young daughter at Woolworths in Pretoria's plush Brooklyn Mall when he felt a tap on his shoulder. His wife, Vanitha, was facing Gordhan and could see who was behind him. Her face went cold, and she turned away and walked off with the child.

Gordhan turned around to see a face that took his mind back through the years to 1990, and a very different set of circumstances. The man was Karl Durr – formerly Lieutenant Karl Durr of the notorious South African Police Security Branch in Durban.

Durr had been one of two Security Branch officers from Durban assigned to interrogate Gordhan after the Operation Vula crackdown. The other was Inspector Frans Bothma.

On Friday evening, 13 July 1990, a day after his arrest in Overport, Gordhan had been taken to Newcastle police station cells. He'd been allowed to spend some of the R100 he had on him on a tracksuit top but still remembers the Newcastle cell as being 'bloody cold'.

Two days later he was taken to Bethlehem, to the district surgeon's offices there, to go through 'some stupid examination', after which he ended up in a cell at the local Security Branch offices. There was one other Operation Vula detainee already there – Raymond Lalla, who would, ironically, go on to become a lieutenant-general in the post-apartheid South African Police Service.

The reason why Bethlehem was chosen remains unclear. Police giving evidence at the TRC said there weren't enough cells at CR Swart in Durban to accommodate all the Section 29 detainees, but Gordhan countered that it was because from 1891 the then Orange Free State – at the time an independent Boer republic – had not allowed South Africans of Indian descent to live there, a regulation that had lived on during the apartheid era. Gordhan said taking him to an area traditionally hostile to Indians was part of a series of steps designed to intimidate him.

Gordhan had been detained twice before and had become familiar with Security Branch tactics. In 1981 he'd been detained for 161 days, during which chunks of his beard were ripped out by a Security Branch officer who was interrogating him: 'He had rough scissors. He attempted to cut … when the scissors couldn't cut, he would pull the beard,' Gordhan remembers. After being released from this period of detention he was placed under house arrest and banned for a year. In 1985 he was again detained, for five weeks.

This time, Durr and Bothma would spend their weekends in Durban, driving the nearly 400km to and from the Free State town every week. On Sundays Gordhan's wife Vanitha would meet Durr at CR Swart police station. 'She used to meet him and he would decide whether a packet of Marie biscuits could be accepted or not, whether a bar of chocolate would be allowed,' says Gordhan. 'If he wanted to be nasty, he'd say, "I'm not taking anything this weekend." If he wanted to be nice, he'd take a set of clothes to be washed and collect another set of clothes to bring back. And he treated her horribly.'

Durr and Bothma routinely interrogated Gordhan but after

nearly a month they'd got no joy: he remained determined not to provide any information.

Then Lieutenant-Colonel Hentie Botha entered the picture.

Moe Shaik, in his 2020 book *The ANC Spy Bible: Surviving Across Enemy Lines*, describes Botha as a 'slim man with a compact, athletic body'. He had a 'youthful baby-face topped with well-groomed hair' and 'bore a striking resemblance' to the actor Richard Dean Anderson, best known for playing the lead character in the television series *MacGyver*.

Shaik describes Botha as a 'skilled interrogator' who had 'long since lost his humanity'. He recounts an incident in which his brother Yunus had some sort of instrument inserted in his rectum by a doctor while Botha was interrogating him. With every denial, the instrument was plunged deeper 'and turned to cause maximum trauma and pain'.

Gordhan today describes Botha as a 'vicious character' and there's plenty of evidence to support this description, including the torture of Shaik and others, and the murder of Charles Ndaba.

In the Bethlehem Security Branch offices in 1990 Gordhan was about to find out how vicious the Security Branch officer was.

Botha told the TRC he travelled to Bethlehem to try to get from Gordhan the identity of a policeman who'd secretly been giving information to the ANC. The police mole was known by the ANC underground as 'The Owl'.

In Bethlehem a friendly policeman had begun supplying newspapers to Gordhan, so he was up to speed on current events and could give answers to Botha that revealed nothing more than had already been made public.

Later, at the TRC, Botha said, 'Mr Gordhan did not cooperate in any way with regard to the questions which were put to him regarding the identity of the mole. He denied any knowledge of who the person was and it became clear that Gordhan would not provide any information, and I ceased the interrogation.'

Gordhan, pointing out that Botha's interrogation had been brief and cursory, says the policeman's real and 'only purpose was to break my spirits', and the Security Branch officer quickly turned to assault.

At about 5.30pm the sun began to set in the room in which Gordhan had been questioned. Botha left the room and two other policemen 'asked me to stand up and face the window of that particular office. [They] then walked out of the office,' Gordhan told the TRC during cross-examination of Botha, who had applied for amnesty. Within about thirty seconds a hood had been placed over Gordhan's head, and he was wrapped in a blanket which was tied around him, probably with rope.

During questioning of Botha at the TRC, Gordhan said: 'I was dropped very gently to the ground. The hood was lifted to cover only my eyes so I could only recognise you by your voice, and you then used ... some rubber or plastic material to suffocate me by covering my nose and mouth.'

Gordhan struggled but was restrained. Bothma told the TRC that he and another policeman had helped to hold Gordhan down during the assault. He said that Gordhan hadn't been cooperative 'since the start of his detention ... we had to struggle to obtain his name and surname from him.'

Botha told the TRC, 'I worked with Mr Gordhan and he was not prepared to provide any information with regard to the mole. Consequently I decided to use a method of coercion to oblige him to provide information to me. The reason why I assaulted Mr Gordhan was in order to obtain the information from him which would be of tremendous value to the Security Branch at that stage.'

Botha denied he'd been acting on orders. 'No, [the decision to torture Gordhan] was my decision. It was my opinion that this would be the only method in which to coerce Mr Gordhan to give the information.'

The exchanges between Gordhan and Botha at the TRC were sharp, with the policeman claiming the torture had lasted only minutes, and Gordhan saying it had been much longer than that, more like thirty to fifty minutes.

Responding to a question from Gordhan, Botha said, 'Your attitude was aggressive and one of arrogance, and you did not want to cooperate, and my decision was to use violence to extract information from you.'

During the torture, Gordhan was subjected to 'extreme aggression', swearing and abuse. Botha was in a 'violent mood' and warned Gordhan that he might not see his family again.

Asked by Gordhan if he'd intended to kill him, Botha told the TRC the threat about not seeing his family again was a 'general statement … in order to influence you that I was serious'.

Asked by a TRC lawyer whether the torture had had any physical effect on Gordhan, Botha said, 'I could not see whether it had any physical effect on him. All that I could observe was that Mr Gordhan was a very aggressive person and his attitude was negative regarding the questions which were put to him. If I had to evaluate, I would say that the suffocation had absolutely no effect on him.'

Gordhan remembers those events clearly. 'I was quite determined that I wouldn't tell him [Botha] a damn thing, he could do what he liked. Those were moments when you have to decide: you either give in to his crap or you take an attitude which says you can do what you like. And if it's the end of me, well, that's bad luck, it's the end of me.'

Today, Gordhan points out, 'A moral crisis that every single activist in detention would have faced is: how much do you tell the security police? And at what cost and maybe what benefit?'

Maharaj says his view was that if a comrade was arrested and tortured, he or she should try to hold out for 48 hours. 'And if you can't hold on for 48 hours, then try for 24 hours. But after that, I'm not asking you to let them kill you for the information. I've been through torture, I accept that people will break down and [you should] rather give information before you break down so that you control the information. After that, I have no grudge. I have no grudge.'

After assaulting Gordhan, Botha turned his attention to Lalla but stopped the assault when the detainee suffered an asthma attack while being suffocated.

✦

At the TRC hearing, Gordhan argued that the assaults were the result of a 'culture that developed among some of the policemen at that time ... that it was as a result of almost an habitual practice as opposed to a well thought-out decision'.

Botha disagreed with this, but in its final report the TRC pointed out that it had received thousands of statements alleging torture and it was 'clear that it was the norm for agents of the state to carry out various torture practices on those who were in their custody'. Turning to the issue of accountability, the report noted that 'the former government conceded that torture occurred, but claimed that it represented the actions of a few renegade policemen'.

However, Leon Wessels, the NP's former deputy minister of police, admitted to the TRC 'that it was not possible to deny knowledge of torture'. He testified that 'it was foreseen that under those circumstances people would be detained, people would be tortured. Everybody in the country knew that people were tortured.'

The TRC noted, 'Given the statements of victims, their families, the testimony of amnesty applicants ... and others on the practice of torture, and the condonation and cover-up by superior officers when cases went horribly wrong, there can be no doubt that torture was widespread, well known and tolerated.'

In damning findings, the TRC said, 'Condonation of torture by superior officers was further evidenced by the fact that most well-known torturers were promoted to higher positions … Magistrates and judges seldom protected detainees or ruled in their favour, even though a pattern of abuse was familiar … More distressing is the fact that many judges and magistrates continued to accept the testimony of detainees, despite the fact that most of them knew that the testimony had been obtained under interrogation and torture while in detention. In this way, the judiciary and the magistracy indirectly sanctioned this practice and, together with the leadership of the former apartheid state, must be held accountable for its actions.'

Botha himself told his amnesty hearing 'a stage arose during the activities of the Security Branch where we worked outside the law but believed that we were acting correctly and that it was necessary – that we had to do what we had to do, and consequently [used] violence with interrogation.'

Gordhan argued that in the hearing Botha had shown no 'serious remorse' and his approach to reconciliation was 'wanting in sincerity'. Nonetheless, in March 1999, the TRC granted amnesty for the assaults on Gordhan and Lalla to Botha, Bothma and Durr – who'd been present in the room when Gordhan was assaulted but claimed that he'd only been there to take notes.

✦

After several more weeks in detention, Gordhan and the other Operation Vula activists who'd been detained were charged with terrorism.

The charge sheet read:

> During the period July 1988 to July 1990 and at Durban, Kwa-Mashu, Umlazi, La Lucia, Tongaat, Sydenham, Avoca, Reservoir Hills, Greenwood Park, Kenville and Chatsworth in the Province of Natal, Soshanguve, Yeoville, Parkhurst, Berea, Parktown, Lyttelton, Melrose North and Johannesburg in the Province of Transvaal, and also at other places within the Republic of South Africa and elsewhere, the accused unlawfully and with intent to overthrow or endanger the State authority in the Republic:
>
> (1) performed acts which were aimed at causing, bringing about, promoting or contributing towards acts or threats of violence, or alternatively, attempted or took steps to perform such acts; and/or
>
> (2) conspired each with the other and with other persons to bring about or perform such acts or to aid in the bringing about or performance thereof; and/or
>
> (3) incited, instigated, commanded, aided, advised, encouraged or procured other persons to bring about or perform such acts.

There were also 'alternative charges' under the Arms and Ammunition Act against Pravin Gordhan, for the alleged possession of a Makarov pistol, a limpet mine, detonators and ammunition.

Gordhan believes the police had planted the weaponry in the flat. 'I had some political material there, but never kept any arms there,' he says today. 'They moved this wardrobe and underneath were these things. So I said, "I didn't put that there." So they obviously planted this stuff – that's the only way it could have got there.'

The NP responded with outrage when news of Operation Vula was first made public, accusing the ANC of bad faith during talks the two parties were having about a formal negotiation process. The NP feared that the ANC planned to overthrow the government while pretending to negotiate.

The ANC, for its part, had kept Operation Vula in place as an insurance policy in case the talks failed. The party's then president, Oliver Tambo, argued that it shouldn't be deprived of 'our weapons of struggle' until it was clear the negotiation process had developed an unstoppable momentum.

In 1991, with many of the Operation Vula operatives now involved in the Codesa negotiations, they were given indemnity from prosecution by the state as part of an agreement in which the ANC suspended its 'armed activities'.

Gordhan developed hypertension after the Operation Vula detention and torture, but otherwise seems to have put the episode behind him, pointing out that many others suffered more severe torture or were killed.

Seeing Durr again in 1999 obviously brought back unpleasant memories 'but by then we'd learned the art of forgiveness, I suppose', he says drily.

But what did they discuss in Woolworths that day – a setting in sharp contrast to the cold and bare cells of the Bethlehem Security Branch offices?

'Just banalities, you know. He was embarrassed.'

7

The Dawn of Democracy

In late 1989 a buzz started among activists that several high-profile Robben Island political prisoners might be on the brink of release, remembers Pravin Gordhan. Before that, he and his comrades sometimes proclaimed that they would celebrate freedom in their lifetimes, but even they weren't convinced. 'It certainly came sooner than we thought [it would],' he says today.

On 15 October 1989, long-term Robben Island inmates Walter Sisulu, Ahmed Kathrada, Jafta Masemola, Raymond Mhlaba, Wilton Mkwayi, Andrew Mlangeni, Elias Motsoaledi and Oscar Mpetha were freed.

'That, then, of course, changed the momentum completely,' says Gordhan.

It did, and South Africa experienced an astonishing roller-coaster ride over the following four and a half years. On 2 February 1990, then president FW de Klerk announced that the ANC, the Pan Africanist Congress (PAC) and the SACP would be unbanned, and that Nelson Mandela – by then the world's most famous political prisoner – would be released. Nine days later, Mandela made his historic walk out of Victor Verster prison, near Paarl, after 27 years of being jailed.

Negotiations to bring an end to apartheid were about to begin, but it was to be anything but a smooth road. A blizzard of extraordinary developments engulfed the country on its journey to democracy: many were encouraging, others horrifying. Several seemed designed to halt the negotiations at critical phases: news reporters who covered the talks recall breakthroughs almost inevitably being followed by crises that threatened the process.

Stories on the negotiations and related developments were plastered across the front pages of newspapers every day of the week. As is the nature of news, the biggest headlines were reserved for the most chilling events. These included the Boipatong Massacre on 17 June 1992, in which 46 residents of the Gauteng township were killed when local hostel dwellers went on the rampage. The hostels were aligned to the Inkatha Freedom Party (IFP) and the clashes had roots in the conflict between that party and the ANC, but there were widespread suspicions that the police had played a hand in the violence that night by transporting and supporting IFP members.

Four days later, the ANC pulled out of negotiations, citing the violence at Boipatong and other places, and suggesting that the state was negotiating in bad faith. It launched a campaign of 'rolling mass action' – consecutive mass protests around the country.

On 7 September of the same year, 29 people died in the Bisho Massacre when Ciskei Defence Force soldiers opened fire on some 80 000 ANC supporters who were marching on Bisho, then the Ciskei capital.

On 26 September, apparently spurred on by the events at Bisho, the government and the ANC agreed on a 'record of understanding' which persuaded negotiators back to the table. It included commitments on a constitutional assembly, an interim government, political prisoners, hostels, dangerous weapons and mass action.

On 10 April 1993, Chris Hani, the leader of the SACP and

chief of staff of MK, was shot dead outside his home in Dawn Park, Boksburg. He was extremely popular among grassroots supporters for his charisma and derring-do.

Hani's neighbour, an Afrikaans woman called Margareta Harmse, had reversed out of her driveway just as a man had jumped into his car and fled the scene. She noted his car number plate, and went back inside and called the police. Janusz Waluś, a Polish immigrant, was arrested soon afterwards.

The murder gave rise to riots, and fears that the country would descend into widespread violence. Nelson Mandela addressed the nation in a bid to calm tensions. At the time his remarks were widely described as presidential, but with hindsight they were also the moment when he asserted his presence as the rightful leader of the country. 'Tonight I am reaching out to every single South African, black and white, from the very depths of my being,' he said. 'A white man, full of prejudice and hate, came to our country and committed a deed so foul that our whole nation now teeters on the brink of disaster. A white woman, of Afrikaner origin, risked her life so that we may know, and bring to justice, this assassin.'

He continued, 'Now is the time for all South Africans to stand together against those who, from any quarter, wish to destroy what Chris Hani gave his life for – the freedom of all of us.'

The assassination galvanised negotiators, who soon agreed on an election date – 27 April of the following year.

On 11 March 1994, hundreds of far-right Afrikaner Weerstands-beweging (AWB) supporters poured into Bophuthatswana in a quixotic attempt to quell an uprising against the homeland leader Lucas Mangope, who'd backed the right and other parties opposed to the negotiations – including the IFP – in the multi-party Concerned South Africans Group (COSAG).

They were quickly sent packing, but a grim incident broadcast on television had a dampening effect on the more cavalier right-wing elements: it showed three injured and pleading AWB members sprawled next to their car being shot dead by a Bophuthatswana policeman.

On 28 March thousands of Zulu supporters of King Goodwill Zwelethini converged on the Johannesburg city centre and engaged in a series of running battles with ANC combatants. More than thirty people died on the day, including ten shot dead by ANC security outside its Shell House headquarters.

On 19 April, after days of separate talks, the IFP agreed to contest the elections – to be held in just eight days.

Over the following week several bombs went off – the dying throes of the right-wing resistance. One outside the ANC's regional headquarters in central Johannesburg killed nine people and injured 92.

For most of this time – apart from during the months after the Boipatong Massacre – talks were taking place, either in the initial Codesa, or in the subsequent Multiparty Negotiating Forum (MPNF), or in smaller, informal meetings.

The negotiations venue was the so-called World Trade Centre in Kempton Park, not far from Johannesburg's main airport, now named after Oliver Tambo but then still rejoicing in the name Jan Smuts International Airport. The World Trade Centre is less grand than its name suggests: it's basically a massive warehouse with some conference rooms and offices on the upper level. It was in one of these rooms that the negotiators would meet for plenary sessions.

The talks had been kicked off by two significant agreements, the Groote Schuur Minute (the 4 May 1990 agreement between Nelson

Mandela and FW de Klerk on the resolution of the prevailing climate of violence and intimidation, as well as on stability and a peaceful process of negotiations) and the Pretoria Minute (the 6 August 1990 agreement that included the suspension of the ANC's armed struggle and the end of the state of emergency). This had then been given momentum by the National Peace Accord, signed on 14 September 1991 by 26 organisations, establishing multiparty conflict-resolution structures at the community level.

Each of these had removed significant stumbling blocks to the talks, and they had the cumulative effect of tying the major players into the process.

Roelf Meyer, the minister of constitutional affairs and communication in De Klerk's cabinet, was chosen to be the government's chief negotiator at the talks. 'There were moments when we all were in doubt, I think,' he says today. 'But, you know, those of us who were so deeply involved never gave up in our minds. We weren't prepared to give up, despite all the challenges that the process came across. We couldn't go back to the point before we started. But it was because of that passionate commitment on both sides of the aisle [that the negotiations succeeded]. When I say both, it was essentially between the ANC and the National Party government, because the one had the power and the other one was entitled to the power.'

Those 'deeply involved' included Pravin Gordhan, sent to the talks as a delegate for the ANC-aligned NIC and among those who were profoundly committed to the process. 'He was the one who stood out because of his competence, the way in which he was totally analytical about matters,' says Meyer.

He adds that Gordhan was excellent at finding solutions to the many disputes and disagreements that popped up in the process. 'There were two people in that category ... the other one was [SACP leader] Joe Slovo.'

Nonetheless, Meyer recalls Gordhan as initially being prickly and difficult to get along with. 'When Pravin and I first met, it was with certain images in each other's minds, of course. I mean, he was Communist Party and I was a member of the apartheid regime. And so in our minds I guess we were completely against each other,' he says.

Meyer describes Gordhan as having been 'very abrasive'. 'He's a natural rebel ... so that is how I came to know him. [He] was a real activist. Even now, sometimes, when I speak to him, he will say that he's still an activist. But he came from that background and as a result he was probably a little bit more antagonistic [towards] people in the regime than many of his colleagues.'

As an example, Meyer recalls the ANC's Joe Modise as 'immediately reaching out – and I was reaching out – despite the fact that we knew exactly who we were and where we were coming from'. Gordhan, however, kept Meyer and his colleagues at arm's length.

Perhaps Gordhan had cause to be wary when he arrived at the negotiating table. In 1991, soon after having been given temporary immunity from prosecution in terms of the Groote Schuur Minute, and in preparation for negotiations, he'd noticed a hole in the ceiling of his new duplex home in Durban – it looked like a foot had broken through the ceiling from above. 'So that raised some question marks,' says Gordhan. 'My wife got Moe Shaik and company to come along. They went into the ceiling and they found bugs in two of the bedrooms.'

It was later established that the Security Branch had rented the unit next door, crossing over into the adjoining unit – Gordhan's – in the ceiling, and planting the bugs. 'They still wanted to know where the arms were from the Vula period,' Gordhan says. 'Ja, so that's the irony: amnesty of some kind in March '91, and this incident probably around July '91.'

It was in November of that year that Gordhan was called to

Johannesburg and asked to represent the NIC at the negotiating table. The first plenary session of the Codesa talks was held in December, and in January of 1992 Gordhan was appointed chair of the negotiating process's planning committee – a body that was central to progress in the talks.

It was in this committee that the principle of majority rule had to be canvassed. Gordhan remembers 'proposal after proposal from the Nats about how to dilute [it]'.

In March 1993 he was appointed an MPNF chair and had to approach his task with a different mindset. 'But, ja, you learn. I came from a very militant background so [had] to adapt to a situation where you've got to talk, and you've got to look for the art of the possible, and you've got to think quickly on your feet, reach compromise formulations, which would keep everybody on board without appearing to be one-sided. And that's what being the chair demanded. In that context, I couldn't be an ANC chair. I had to be a chair that fairly represented everybody. So what I'd learned from many comrades is how you synthesise different views and look for possible ways out.

'But on much more substantial issues, those didn't happen in the open forum, those happened in closed-door bilaterals where some of the deadlocks were broken … I think the credit there goes to the Mandelas, the Ramaphosas, Valli Moosa, up to a point, but also the constitutional committee that the ANC had set up, which I wasn't privileged to participate in.'

As the process moved forward through its stops and starts, Meyer became 'very much impressed' with Gordhan's qualities and ability. He was surprised that Gordhan was a chemist by profession. 'He came across as a good lawyer, somebody who's very analytical in his mind and his approach.'

As chair of the MPNF forum, 'he wasn't messing around and

playing games', says Meyer; he chaired the meetings 'in such a way that you could rely on him, you trusted him. And he kept his word; he didn't change his mind overnight. As time went on, I started to realise this man's capabilities, and then our relationship started to change into a working relationship.'

❖

There were various constituencies opposed to the negotiations. The most significant and obvious were probably the IFP and the white right wing.

The IFP had been holding out on committing to an election date and contesting the polls over issues centring on the status of the Zulu king and the amount of federal autonomy that would be given to KwaZulu-Natal. Its supporters clashed frequently with ANC followers in the province and elsewhere amid suspicions that a state-sponsored 'third force' was supplying arms and other support to the IFP.

The talks – and Gordhan's role in them – were routinely criticised in the IFP-supporting *Ilanga* newspaper at the time. This became more intense when the 27 April 1994 election date was set. 'I used to be under constant attack in the English column that was written by Arthur Konigkramer at the time. [He] would finger me as often as he could.'

On one day during this process a group of about forty women in IFP regalia protested outside the yard of the house where Gordhan and his then pregnant wife were staying. The protest was ostensibly about arms but 'it was clearly due to the decision on the election date'.

The white right-wing parties were also enraged at the direction the talks were taking. On 25 June 1993, an estimated three thousand right-wingers gathered outside the gates to the World Trade Centre in Kempton Park. The protest was led by the Afrikaner Volksfront's General Constand Viljoen – but he hadn't reckoned on the indiscipline of the AWB.

Members of AWB leader Eugène Terre'Blanche's bodyguard unit – who called themselves the Ystergarde (Iron Guard) and dressed entirely in black – began rocking the cars of delegates as they attempted to enter the World Trade Centre premises. Then, suddenly, protesters began pouring through the gate towards the building.

Viljoen, one hand aloft and speaking through a megaphone, tried to stop them but the crowd swept on towards the huge glass doors. In their midst was an armoured troop carrier called a Viper – about the size of a small truck. After a brief stand-off and some scuffles with the police, the Viper was driven by one of the right-wingers through the glass doors, shattering them and scattering glass across the building's foyer. The right-wingers, many by now openly carrying arms, swept through in its wake. The protesters, led by the black-clad Ystergarde, went up an escalator in the reception area and occupied the negotiating chamber.

Delegates headed towards offices deeper in the building where bodyguards were stationed. Gordhan, Meyer, Cyril Ramaphosa, Joe Slovo, Mac Maharaj and several others huddled together in an office. 'All you had was drywall partitioning,' recalls Gordhan. 'One bullet fired there would've [hit] somebody. There were all sorts of phone calls made to make sure that we got additional police assistance. I can't remember how long it lasted but it was an interesting experience.

'[National People's Party leader Amichand] Rajbansi is the one who famously went [back into the chamber] to pick up a pen or something. And they klapped him and his wig shot up.'

Meyer remembers that most of the negotiating council leadership gathered in his office, presumably because his bodyguards were there at the time. 'We were sitting around waiting for the next thing to happen, and then, as we were sitting there, one of the bodyguards came to me and said, "Terre'Blanche is next door in the next office."

'And I got up and I walked over, and there he was. I said, "Hello, Eugène."

'He greeted me.

'And then I said to him: "So what next?"

'And his answer was, "I don't know."'

Besides klapping Rajbansi, Terre'Blanche's supporters were, meanwhile, breaking delegates' name tags in the negotiating chamber and urinating on some of the furniture. Then they held a prayer meeting.

Negotiations between the invaders and the police ended in an agreement that the protesters would be allowed to leave the building peacefully, and soon they did so.

Meyer says the saga 'was overstated in terms of its effect, because it had no effect'. 'If they hadn't come through the front door with the armoured vehicle, [the incursion] would have not been recorded anywhere, I guess. But the mere fact that they rushed through the front door with that armoured vehicle made the difference and made the headlines. The point is, the next day we carried on with our work.'

And was there a hidden hand at play fomenting so-called black-on-black violence – mainly between ANC and IFP supporters – at the time?

Gordhan and many within the ANC ranks thought so. 'What eventually materialised during the Codesa process – the massacre at Boipatong, the so-called black-on-black violence – demonstrated that the regime wasn't as one,' says Gordhan. 'You might remember Hernus Kriel was minister of police when there was this raid into Transkei, and we were actually sitting at the table at the World Trade

Centre, and we heard that a whole lot of people had been killed. And that was his effort at derailing the kind of work that Roelf Meyer and company were doing.'

Meyer is a little more circumspect. He recalls the Transkei incident as a 'big mistake' by South African Defence Force soldiers, who'd been acting on intelligence that PAC members were in the house they were sent to raid. 'Whether that was justifiably aimed at the PAC is another question in itself,' he says, 'but it was a very sad moment for us in the negotiations. Everything came to a standstill. I can recall how [PAC delegate] Benny Alexander was up in arms about it and wanted to stall the whole process as a result of that.

'But, you know, there were other such incidents that one never found out the truth about. In other words: who was behind it? And there were many allegations on an ongoing basis. Boipatong was another such case, as we all can recall, and the ANC until today believe that it was elements within the security forces that operated there – military and police.

'There were people on the right wing who tried to disrupt [the process]. That was very well known. But there were also people within the National Party that wanted to disrupt [it]. We had a serious conservative element within the National Party, you know, and, incidentally, many of them ended up in the DA [Democratic Alliance],' laughs Meyer.

'But many of them wanted to disrupt [the process] for the sake of trying to achieve a "better" deal. Many of them cooperated closely with Buthelezi for that reason. Or with the COSAG parties. Behind the scenes some of them were definitely holding meetings with that group trying to further the aims of COSAG …

'There were definitely people who wanted to stall the process, even up to a very late stage. And there were some who thought we would never reach the point of 27 April 1994.'

But the talks had developed their own momentum and moved inexorably forward. An important factor in this was the adoption of a deadlock-breaking mechanism called 'sufficient consensus'. In essence, it required that the ANC and the South African government agree on an issue for it to be approved, but in practice it required that some of the smaller parties also get on board.

Gordhan says, 'The essential point [was] that I think the Nats originally thought that if they added themselves and a whole lot of homeland governments on one side, they would outnumber the ANC – because it was the ANC, NIC, TIC [Transvaal Indian Congress], and who else on [the ANC] side? But in pure numbers terms, if everybody had to put up their hand and vote, you could be an absolute minority party that could hold up the works. Sufficient consensus, in a sense, remained undescribed, but the bottom line was: do the major players find themselves in a position where they can live with whatever is coming out?'

There were two landmark moments when Gordhan was chairing and had to declare sufficient consensus: on the date of the election and on the subsequent acceptance of the draft constitution.

'When the election date was being discussed, people were getting irritated with me because I gave the IFP a lot of rope and time – tea breaks and more breaks,' remembers Gordhan. 'And my own comrades were getting impatient: "Come on, man, just declare it sufficient consensus." I took a little bit of extra time – maybe an hour and a half more – but nobody could say I was being unfair; nobody could say they didn't have an opportunity to articulate a different view. And eventually we did declare sufficient consensus.

'When the final form of the draft constitution was being put forward to the plenary, I had to declare sufficient consensus again,' says Gordhan. 'But this time there was much less noise.'

Meyer says Gordhan's interpretation of the mechanism was

masterful. 'It mostly boiled down to how the chairperson was inter-preting it. And he was, to my mind, the best at it. It was for the same reason that I was very disappointed that he didn't become speaker of the national assembly [after 1994]. I thought he would have been a natural speaker.'

◈

In the early hours of the morning of 18 November 1993 the MPNF adopted the interim constitution.

South Africa went to the polls for its first democratic elections on 27 April 1994. Nearly twenty million people voted on that extraordinary day.

8

The Higher Purpose

Expertise in tax matters is the one qualification you'd think would be crucial to head up a revenue service – and yet Pravin Gordhan is no tax expert. At least, he wasn't in 1999, when he was appointed commissioner of SARS.

And yet, when he left SARS a decade later, the service was, according to *The New York Times*, 'an extraordinary triumph'. With Gordhan at the helm, SARS had managed to get millions of South Africans to do the unthinkable: pay their taxes – and, more miraculous still, do so happily. 'In a barometer of support for the fledgling new government, tax collections rose year after year, eventually surpassing some benchmarks in much richer, more established democracies, including the United States,' *The New York Times* stated.

This was all the more remarkable considering that when Gordhan took over the tax authority, dodging tax was a national pastime. In fact, for many people, avoiding tax was a legitimate form of protest against the apartheid government. Five years into democracy, the political act of tax defiance remained a bad habit that was proving difficult to break.

The post-1994 government's priority was to address the country's extreme inequality and reduce its rampant poverty. To do this, it needed to build houses, schools and clinics, and provide water and electricity to people who'd been neglected by the apartheid government. It needed a large public purse to fund its ambitious reconstruction and development programme, which meant its tax revenue service had to operate effectively and efficiently.

The pre-1994 revenue service had been in disarray. Its management was weak, its processes archaic, there were very few systems in place, and revenue collection was haphazard. The ANC-led government launched the Katz Commission to make recommendations to overhaul the tax system so that political liberation could be coupled with economic liberation. After an extensive review, the commission produced an interim report on which the autonomous SARS was established, unifying inland revenue and customs and excise into one entity.

Trevor Manuel, the then minister of finance, wanted someone who had good political nous and who could streamline the organisation to head it up. He chose Gordhan, who had a solid reputation as a sharp operator and a brilliant strategist on both political and economic matters. His organisational qualities had been evident during the struggle days and he'd been recognised as a master tactician in the Codesa negotiations. He'd also excelled as a backbencher in parliament and had played a crucial role in getting the first local-government elections off the ground.

For Momo Momoniat, who was working in the treasury, Gordhan, a pharmacist by training, wasn't an obvious choice, but was an inspired one. 'SARS needed a visionary, someone to establish the organisation,' he says. 'Pravin may not have been an expert on the tax issues but he knew how to utilise the skills of people and give them the space to function.'

Goolam Aboobaker says Gordhan's pragmatic approach and his

ability to build relationships made him the ideal candidate to head up a technocratic organisation such as SARS.

For Gordhan, who was 50 years old, it meant something new. He'd spent a quarter of a century in activist politics and then five years in parliamentary politics, contributing to important changes in the country. He now had a different set of challenges but as the country's new tax chief he'd continue to serve the public. Shortly after his appointment he told the historian Padraig O'Malley that his new job would also allow him to spend time with his wife Vanitha, a former community activist from [then] Natal, and his two daughters.

Gordhan's task was to restore legitimacy to the institution; to broaden the tax base by bringing more taxpayers into the net; and to grow the revenue base by cutting the exemptions and exceptions that existing taxpayers were using as loopholes.

For Gordhan, walking into SARS in March 1998 – when he joined the organisation as deputy commissioner; he was appointed commissioner the following year – was like walking into the old South Africa. It was about eighty percent white; at management level it was just about a hundred percent white. In fact, Gordhan was the first black person in a senior-management position in the institution.

He wanted to transform SARS and give black South Africans an opportunity to enter the institution and grow in it. Within months he introduced a programme of reforms called Siyakha, which means 'we are building' in isiZulu, and he set up a parallel, second-level exco to give younger black managers an opportunity at the top level. He brought in people who could make a difference – one of them was his struggle comrade Ivan Pillay, who joined SARS as chief officer for enforcement and compliance risk, before being appointed its deputy commissioner.

According to Pillay, from the moment Gordhan walked into the organisation he 'owned the job'. 'You own your role first and foremost. You try to understand what the job is about, what it demands, and you set about doing it,' says Pillay. 'Pravin wasn't distracted during his period at SARS. He lived a simple life. If your life is too cluttered, it becomes blurred.' Gordhan's focus, he says, was razor-sharp.

Peter Richer, who joined SARS in the role of risk management and strategy, says Gordhan brought his activist background to his role. He didn't consult managerial textbooks but drew from his experience in mobilising communities in the way he ran the tax authority. In other words, Gordhan ran SARS like a political campaign. (Years later, just before Gordhan left SARS, his former struggle comrade Mandla Nkomfe bumped into him at the airport and asked him what the secret was to SARS's success. Gordhan told him that it was because he was using the same methods at SARS that had been used in the UDF.)

Gordhan knew that above all else he had to change people's mindsets about paying tax. He introduced the concept of the 'higher purpose' – that the whole future of the country rested on having an efficient tax service – which he would push every time he spoke to staff and in management meetings, and he travelled around the country to stress his message. Tax was the foundation for building a developmental state – and without an efficient tax regime and without compliance, there wouldn't be satisfactory health care or decent schools or proper houses.

Gordhan also believed that if there was tax compliance, citizens would start to comply with the law in general, which would help move the country from the anarchy of the apartheid period to a law-based society.

'Pravin spent a lot of time talking directly to staff and would keep talking about the higher purpose,' says Richer. 'What he was trying to do was to lift SARS out of a sense of civil-service drudgery into an idea that the whole future of the country rested on having an efficient tax service, and also a level of compliance.'

Gordhan wanted to build compliance by explaining to people why they pay tax, what tax is, where the money goes and how it actually benefits them. This sentiment was reflected in the revenue service's advertising at the time, which thanked taxpayers – not for paying their taxes, but for providing houses, clinics and schools.

'Back in that period,' says Richer, 'we could literally say that the tax money had built so many thousands of houses, so many clinics, so many universities ... everything was being related to this provision of services. This was the concept of the higher purpose. We weren't just public servants, we were campaigners for this higher purpose.'

Pillay says the 'higher purpose' message caught on well. 'People understood that we were there not just doing a piece of work, we were there to build up an efficient and an effective revenue authority, so that resources would be available for a democratic government to utilise, to address our legacy.'

Johann van Loggerenberg, who ran the tax agency's high-risk investigations unit, says that SARS was about radical economic transformation (RET). 'I know "economic freedom" and "radical economic transformation" are big words today, but they used those terms then. "Radical" can mean many things, but to me it means speedy, as soon as you can do it, because you don't [want to] waste a day. That's what it was. That's how the tax system worked. The more you make, the more you share ... and the people who must make sure you share are SARS.'

In the run-up to democracy, many tax officials of the apartheid or-der had opted for severance packages because they refused to work for the new government. Pillay says that one of the early things that Gordhan's new management team did was to stop the voluntary-severance packages, because the only thing it achieved was that many competent white people, who were confident about their future elsewhere, left.

'What was the point?' Pillay asks. 'It didn't make any sense. I mean, if you want people to pay for apartheid, then actually make them work to break the legacy of apartheid. Don't kick them out. When you do that, you're actually rewarding them.'

According to Pillay, Gordhan made it very clear that no person would lose their job because of their colour, and the opposite was also true: no person would be tolerated for not performing, no matter their colour. The new management created an environment in SARS where people's past wasn't an issue, and where gender, race and sexual orientation didn't count against them.

'We found a fair number of gay Afrikaners in SARS who were suppressed and who welcomed us because we gave them that freedom,' Pillay recalls. 'The same applied to women. When we got there, sixty-five or seventy percent of the staff were women, and hardly any of them were in the senior structures. They were our natural allies, and once they saw that we were serious and honest, and that we were trying to do this the right way, we had less and less friction. As SARS progressed with less and less friction, it became much easier to do things.'

Gordhan knew that the skills required to run a tax administration weren't simple and that SARS needed to retain the old guard's expertise. 'The law alone is very complex,' Richer confirms. 'Most state departments administer maybe up to five different laws but SARS administers sixty-something different laws. Pravin was very conscious of the need to retain the very experienced tax professionals, particularly on the legal side, but was emphatic that they had to commit to the higher purpose. There was no space for them if they still had an apartheid mindset. He wouldn't compromise on that.'

Gordhan kept professionals from the old receiver of revenue and the old customs service. 'All the customs officers had white managers, all the tax offices, except for the homelands, had white managers,' he recalls. 'We didn't throw them away. What we said is that you become a specialist and train the younger guys in the tax business, and many of them did it brilliantly. Some of them are still around. We didn't go for this crude idea that the EFF and others are promoting today of blacks in, whites out. Yes, transformation is absolutely key, but you don't produce a VAT [value-added tax] expert in one year. Many of our VAT experts will be fifteen, twenty years in the business.'

But Gordhan also brought in young people and started to train them up and promote them. He introduced black people at all levels of management, and recruited black accountants and lawyers from the private sector into senior positions. SARS had the flexibility to pay people at much higher salary levels than the rest of the public service, so it could recruit people who'd been in senior positions in financial institutions.

Gordhan realised that the easier it was to be compliant, the more likely it was that people would become compliant, and he was adamant that SARS had to be taxpayer-centric and responsive to its clients, the taxpayers. He wanted the revenue service to actually become a 'service'. Officials no longer waited for taxpayers to come to them, but sought them out at large companies, libraries and shopping centres, and helped them file their tax returns. One cold morning in Cape Town, the manager at the Bellville office handed out biscuits and served tea and coffee to chilly taxpayers queuing outside.

A 'filing season' was launched in 2001 with the aim of making life easier for taxpayers by making officials more accessible and by reducing the time people spent in queues. 'We created a whole vibe around the tax season, both within SARS and among the public,' says Gordhan.

The technology he'd inherited was twenty years old, so he introduced a new income-tax system to get SARS online and hired tech boffins to make filing efficient and payment simple. Taxpayers often stopped him to tell him how fantastic their e-filing experience had been.

He encouraged officials to shake off the unimaginative rules-bound public-service culture of the organisation and to think creatively – which is exactly what Campher Serfontein, a bright and committed public servant, did. Gordhan explains that when Sanlam and Old Mutual were demutualised, Serfontein came up with a plan to recoup money from people who owed SARS. He developed a database of all the names of SARS's debtors, which was then delivered to Old Mutual and Sanlam. The financial institutions were told to run the SARS debtors lists against their databases, and the shares of anyone who owed SARS money were seized, which is how tens of thousands of shares ended up in the taxman's hands.

According to a report by the financial news agency Bloomberg, towards the end of each tax year, Gordhan himself would call the chief executives of the country's biggest companies and urge them to settle their tax bills so that he could meet his revenue-collection target. 'He was one our biggest debt collectors,' Gordhan's former assistant Yolisa Pikie told Bloomberg.

'Higher purpose' was the mantra, inclusion was the motto, transformation was the theme and efficiency was the goal.

Richer says that at first Gordhan's campaign-style approach of running the service was 'wonderful', because it created momentum and energy, and staff felt like they were part of changing things. But there came a point where there was a need for more managerial solidity.

'The old-timers in the legal department and the auditors who didn't come from [a political] background couldn't understand this style of management. The public service is hierarchical, and things go down layer by layer by layer, and you don't have somebody standing up in a rally and saying, "Okay, comrades, march."'

Running an activist-style campaign within a public-service environment created difficulties, and Gordhan soon started to bed down proper systems and organisational management effects, and develop good succession plans.

Gordhan says SARS learned from the Swedes and the Australians about a compliance model that had service and enforcement as the two arms of its approach – and he adopted education as a third one, because he was aware that in the South African situation lots of people weren't tax literate.

He sums up the SARS strategy: 'If you were a good taxpayer, you received good service. If you were a lousy taxpayer, you were klapped in whatever way was necessary.'

The banks got a klap. Gordhan discovered that they'd been paying an average of zero tax. 'We just put the chief executives around a table and said, "These are your tax contributions over the last couple of years. That must change."' Five or six years later, the banks were paying an average of eighteen percent tax.

While the service was reaching out to taxpayers, it was also flexing its enforcement muscle. 'We took on the big guys,' Gordhan says. He told the accounting firms to stop playing games with the tax system and clamped down on the kingpins in the electronic 'grey goods' syndicates, which imported and sold products outside of official channels. It set up the high-risk investigations unit to focus on tax, customs and excise contraventions by organised-crime syndicates, and it also aggressively pursued tax dodgers. 'The enforcement capability was an attempt to make SARS more transparent,' says Richer.

Gordhan knew there had to be examples, but the examples were never arbitrary. The methods by which cases were selected had always been fuzzy, explains Richer. 'In the old service, it seemed to be down to individual officials, who would cherry-pick who to go after. One of the functions of building an effective risk department was to risk-evaluate all taxpayers and actually build a risk profile around groups of taxpayers or individual taxpayers, and on the basis of that risk profile, to choose who to audit and who to investigate, so that there was an objective basis.'

Gordhan wanted to give people a chance to cooperate, and retracing cases that ended up in the courts show that those who were in the tax agency's crosshairs were all given warnings before legal action was launched.

One of the highest-profile battles Gordhan had during his reign at SARS was that with billionaire businessman Dave King. Gordhan made numerous attempts to reach a settlement with King. 'King would renege on the settlement, and only then would he get taken to court,' says Richer. 'King was playing for time, but it does show Pravin's attitude.'

Former cabinet minister Derek Hanekom had admired Gordhan when they were both involved in the UDF during the 1980s but they'd worked in different regions and hadn't had much contact with each other. He got to know Gordhan when an associate who had tax woes asked him if he could arrange a meeting with the tax chief so the parties could reach an amicable settlement.

'I played a little mediation role there, and had these discussions with Pravin, and we gelled almost immediately. He didn't question my motives or agenda, and acknowledged that it would clearly be in everyone's interest if the matter could be settled. What came through very strongly was that Pravin's a tough negotiator and quite uncompromising on principles, but very strategic in approach. In other words, any compromise would certainly be governed by bottom-line principles and there would have to be a genuine case for it.

'The person who owed the revenue service a lot of money made an interesting comment. He said, "Right now I'm at war with Pravin and Pravin is after me, but [from the point of view of] a business-person, Pravin is the best news that business could ever have had because it's exactly somebody like Pravin that we want as the commissioner of taxes. I disagree with him legally and so I'm taking him on, but I'm taking on a person whom I respect very deeply."'

In any event, says Hanekom, the two parties didn't manage to strike a deal because Gordhan wasn't prepared to find the easiest route out of the impasse. 'Pravin was prepared to listen but he wasn't prepared to compromise on principles because it was taxpayers' money that ought to be ploughed back into the economy.'

Gordhan was firm that what was owed to the fiscus was owed to the fiscus.

✦

When Gordhan left SARS ten years later to take over from Trevor Manuel as finance minister, SARS was considered a world-class organisation and was regarded as one of the country's best-functioning public institutions. Under Gordhan's watch, SARS had become, in the words of tax guru Judge Dennis Davis, 'the jewel in the state crown'.

The tax authority's turnaround was praised by the World Bank and highlighted as a success story by Princeton University and other leading business schools.

The stats confirm that the accolades were deserved: in the decade

Gordhan led the organisation, the number of people paying income tax increased from 2,6 million to 4,1 million, and tax revenues jumped from R184 billion to R558 billion, while corporate tax and personal income tax were cut.

The New York Times quoted government records that showed that from 1994 to 2010, the number of people paying taxes nearly quadrupled – remarkably, people actually wanted to pay tax because they felt it was their patriotic duty.

Momoniat says that under Gordhan SARS collected more money than had been budgeted for every year. 'Pravin used his skills to organise SARS into a lean and mean machine,' he says.

Investigative journalist Jacques Pauw writes in his groundbreaking 2017 book *The President's Keepers: Those Keeping Zuma in Power and out of Prison* that even Jacob Zuma had sung the tax collector's praises in a speech in August 2011. 'It is no flattery or exaggeration to single out the South African Revenue Service as one of the most efficient, effective, highly regarded, fair and trusted institutions of state over a prolonged and sustained period,' the then president had stated. 'For without this faith and trust in SARS, our ability as a government to finance our programme of action in meeting the needs of our people would be seriously undermined. It is imperative for SARS to maintain its independence, its values, its moral authority and its objectivity.'

(Pillay would have listened to Zuma's words with disbelief: he'd pleaded with Zuma to settle his tax affairs without success.)

'How somebody who was not a tax expert and who had no experience of managing a big entity could move so smoothly and do it so effectively is a story on its own,' says Derek Hanekom of Gordhan's leapfrog from pharmacist, underground operator and parliamentarian to suddenly being appointed SARS commissioner and heading up a massive institution.

Hanekom points to a number of reasons for Gordhan's success.

'He's an extremely hard worker. He has an amazing strategic mind: he looks at situations, analyses them and puts plans in place, which is how we operated in the underground world. He brought his analytical skill into the institution. He's also a good judge of people, and he brought in people whom he knew he could trust with his life, people who were competent, smart and capable.

'He's not afraid of bringing in the best and having them tell him things that he doesn't want to hear. Pravin listens to people but you have to have a strong case before you can change his mind on anything. He surrounded himself with a really good team, and so if he wasn't a tax expert, he was certainly not afraid to make use of the tax experts, and people with other kinds of expertise that could help strengthen this institution.

'It worked because of those ingredients: hard worker, brilliant analyst and strategic thinker, and unafraid to bring the best people in to help fix and build the institution.'

Three of the highly skilled, extremely capable and dedicated people Gordhan brought into SARS were Ivan Pillay, Peter Richer and Johann van Loggerenberg, who have their own theories about the success at SARS.

According to Pillay, Gordhan knows what he wants and doesn't rest until he gets it. 'He worked very long hours and he got us to work very long hours in order to deliver. He was a taskmaster and he was a pacesetter. He is very, very careful about anything that he does, and he's likely to check and check and counter-check those things until people have given him a level of confidence, and then he will make the decision.'

Pillay points out that Gordhan is pedantic, doesn't suffer fools and gets 'impatient with any BS'.

What Pillay describes as Gordhan's pedantry, Richer calls Gordhan's 'eye for details' – although, Richer concedes, he sometimes felt that Gordhan occasionally drilled too deep and became a micro-manager, which frustrated Richer, who at times felt like they were tripping over each other. 'I understand it. When you're trying to turn around an enormous agency like SARS, you have to have an eye for the details,' he says, adding that Gordhan never made arbitrary decisions; there was always a reason and it was always thought out. 'For somebody like me, who's very into strategy and very into big-picture risk profiling, [working with Gordhan] was a dream,' says Richer.

A characteristic of Gordhan's that stood out above all else for Richer was his integrity.

He adds that Gordhan always emphasised that tax was there to do something – build houses, schools and clinics, and so forth – which is why, years later, when he was minister of finance, he was so horrified by the beginning of the looting. 'He could see that the moment that started to happen, it was going to undermine compliance. People weren't going to have faith in a tax system that raised money to be squandered,' says Richer.

In his 2016 book *Rogue: The Inside Story of SARS's Elite Crime-Busting Unit*, Van Loggerenberg writes how much he was inspired by Gordhan's leadership. He quotes a letter by then finance minister Trevor Manuel describing Gordhan's career as commissioner: 'It is not a leadership that emanates from being elected into positions of authority, rather it is a leadership strength that is a rare combination of an incredibly fine and organised mind, a deep passion to effect change in the lives of all and a determination to see every project to its conclusion. That is the story of [Gordhan's] entire adult life.'

In 2014, five years after Gordhan left SARS, the *Sunday Times* ran a series of sensational stories, each more salacious and sinister than the one before. The bold headlines splashed across its front pages contained tales of wild abuse at the revenue service, with scandalous details of spies, jilted lovers, sexual intrigue, blondes, bugs, spying on the president, and establishing a brothel and a rogue unit.

At the centre of these allegations was Van Loggerenberg's high-risk investigations unit, which had been rebranded by the *Sunday Times* – and subsequently a host of other publications and news outlets – as the 'rogue unit'. The claim was that it had been illegally established and indulged in illicit activities, including bugging then president Jacob Zuma and running a brothel. (The claims have since been thoroughly discredited.)

The tax commissioner who had replaced Gordhan's successor Oupa Magashula was Zuma appointee Tom Moyane. Within weeks of taking his chair at SARS, Moyane had called on the auditing firm KPMG to investigate. KPMG produced a report confirming that the high-risk investigations unit had 'gone rogue' – and Moyane used the finding to justify a purge that saw the careers of many SARS officials, including those of Pillay, Richer and Van Loggerenberg, go up in smoke, and SARS come apart at the seams.

One sentence in KPMG's report said that Gordhan 'ought to have known of the existence of the unit', which it insisted had been established illegally. It was a sentence that would come back to haunt Gordhan.

The problem is that it was all, to use Pillay's abbreviation, BS.

9

The Making of a Minister

At the beginning of 2009, some five years before the 'rogue unit' headlines shook the country, Gordhan was thinking about his future. He'd been at SARS for ten years and felt it was time to move on. The organisation was solid and was being run by committed and capable people.

At the same time Maria Ramos, the chief executive of Transnet, the country's rail, port and pipeline company headquartered in Johannesburg, had stepped down, and the transport parastatal was looking for someone to replace her. Gordhan decided to throw his hat into the Transnet ring.

There was a rigorous selection process, and after various interviews and psychometric tests the selection committee agreed unanimously that there was only one candidate they could recommend to the then minister of public enterprises Brigitte Mabandla. Pravin Gordhan was offered the job.

When Gordhan informed some people in the ANC that he was considering taking up the Transnet position, he was told not to. The 2009 general election was around the corner, and for Gordhan, being encouraged to walk away from Transnet was a strong signal that he was in line for a position in a new cabinet.

A bitter power struggle within the ANC had seen Jacob Zuma dethrone Thabo Mbeki as the party chief at its national conference in Polokwane in 2007. This meant that Zuma was set to take the reins as South Africa's president after the election, and he would undoubtedly send the Mbeki loyalists packing when he did.

The ANC swept to power, and on the night of Zuma's inauguration, Gordhan's cellphone rang. It was ANC secretary-general Gwede Mantashe, telling him that the new president wanted to see him.

All the men and women who'd received a call from Mantashe that night made their way to Mahlamba Ndlopfu, the president's residence in Pretoria, and waited their turn. Finally, Gordhan was summoned into a meeting with Zuma, the then deputy president Kgalema Motlanthe, and Mantashe, and told he was being appointed minister of finance.

Why did Zuma appoint him specifically into that portfolio? Gordhan shrugs. 'No idea,' he says.

It could have been that although Gordhan didn't have a background in economics, the activist-turned-taxman had gained fiscal credibility from his tenure at SARS. Or it could have been because Zuma thought that he might be able to lean on his former struggle comrade and bend him to his will.

Nevertheless, instead of replacing Ramos at Transnet, Gordhan replaced her husband, Trevor Manuel, as minister of finance.

They were big shoes to fill.

As academics Nico Steytler and Derek Powell point out in a 2010 journal article, 'The impact of the global financial crisis on decentralized government in South Africa', in 2007 South Africa's economy was experiencing its longest period of sustained growth in its history, and future growth was projected. 'The national revenue service had yet again exceeded its revenue collection targets, and the national government was projecting another year of strong growth in public spending on infrastructure and social services. For the first time since 1994, the national government was budgeting for a modest surplus.'

A year later, and just a few months before Gordhan's appointment, the world's economy was on its knees after the subprime bubble burst – predatory private mortgage lending and unregulated markets in the United States led to the global Great Recession of 2007-2009 that cost many their jobs, their savings or their homes.

Gordhan was understandably apprehensive when he was informed about the portfolio he was being handed. 'I sat there,' he recalls. 'It was a heavy responsibility. The wave of the 2008 financial crisis was beginning to hit other parts of the world.'

Gordhan knew he wasn't only walking into a new job, but potentially stepping on an economic landmine. 'There were positives,' he says. 'At that stage, there were some very good officials at the treasury, under good leadership, our banking system was intact, and our regulatory system was among the best in the world.'

The treasury, in general, was seen as a bastion of integrity, good governance and competence, with good technocrats running the show.

There were also negatives. A month after his appointment, Gordhan had to inform parliament that the country would have a R50-billion loss on the revenue side. The economy slid into a recession for the first time in almost two decades and nearly a million jobs were lost in 2009 alone. 'Ja, it was a steep learning curve,' says Gordhan. 'But then, everything has been steep in my life,' he adds, with a wry smile.

❖

For Gordhan, life was comparatively simple in 2009. It was only trying to steer the economy out of choppy financial waters that was keeping him awake at night. He wasn't yet all that worried about his new boss.

'What we know today [about Zuma] didn't even feature in 2009,' he says. 'In the first couple of years of the administration, there were no obvious signals [of state capture].' Some officials saw the new administration as an opportunity to correct what they believed had gone wrong with the Mbeki presidency – specifically, his Aids denialism and his opposition to antiretrovirals.

While many public servants saw Zuma's charisma as a welcome change from the coldness of Mbeki, there were a number of red flags that raised concerns about the new president. Before becoming president, Zuma had already been implicated in a multibillion-dollar arms-deal scandal (the 'strategic defence package', which ended up costing the state over R70 billion, with millions of rands of public money lost to bribery and other irregularities), and had been accused of raping the HIV-positive daughter of a family friend.

'Many of us were sceptical of Zuma,' a senior government official says. 'From the beginning he wanted to break up the treasury. In the Trevor Manuel era, we could be creative and put in place huge growth projects and exciting reforms, but we had to put our plans on the back burner and just maintain what we had when Zuma came in. From day one, we were in defensive mode.'

He adds that Gordhan wasn't naive about Zuma and wasn't an uncritical supporter of him either, but says the new minister was constrained by the delicate power dynamics within the ANC. 'Pravin used to tell us to stop lamenting. It would work on my nerves when he said that, and I would tell him to open his eyes. Pravin knew there were issues with Zuma, but he was able to skirt around them,' the official says.

A former special adviser to Gordhan disagrees with the government official that there were concerns about Zuma from the moment he became president. He says that when Zuma took office, he didn't understand how the levers of finance worked – he knew he could benefit from them, but at that stage he didn't know how. 'It was only when Zuma was pointed at the treasury and at the reserve bank and at SARS [that the president's intentions] became apparent,' says the former adviser.

According to Gordhan, it's clear that the 'nonsense' had already started by the time Barbara Hogan was dismissed as the public enterprises minister in 2010. Hogan would later tell the judicial commission of inquiry into allegations of state capture (chaired by Deputy Chief Justice Raymond Zondo, and frequently shortened to 'the Zondo commission') that Zuma had often interfered in her work and tried to force her to make certain appointments at state-owned enterprises (SOEs).

Zuma summoned her to a meeting with Gwede Mantashe, at which he told her the ANC's national executive committee (NEC) – its ruling body – had decided she ought to be redeployed … to Finland. No explanation was given for her dismissal.

'And then there was silence. I asked if that was all, and they said "yes". I greeted them and left. The president helped me to open the door because it was jammed,' Hogan testified.

Hogan was replaced by Malusi Gigaba, who'd served as deputy minister of home affairs under Mbeki. 'And that,' says Gordhan, 'is when the repurposing of the SOEs actually started, and was followed by Lynne Brown [who replaced Gigaba as public enterprises minister in 2014]. And, of course, today we inherit all that nonsense and what we're doing now is repairing the damage that took place then.'

The report 'Betrayal of the promise: How South Africa is being stolen' released by the State Capacity Research Project in May 2017 confirms Gordhan's view and describes the appointment of Gigaba as the pivotal point in the state-capture project because it initiated the repurposing of SOEs as vehicles for looting.

Gigaba and Brown later testified before the Zondo commission, and both denied any involvement in state capture. At the time of writing, the final report of the commission was still in the making.

Nevertheless, at the time of Hogan's axing, Gordhan says he was still unaware of the scale of the corruption. In fact, he says, in the early years Zuma followed much of the treasury's advice on fiscal approach, and even talked openly in cabinet meetings about the impact of overpayment and corruption.

However, there were a number of allegations of government corruption that were alarming Gordhan, among them a contract in the Free State worth more than R2 billion for the construction of roads that wasn't taking place, and money paid to contractors to build bridges over rivers so children in Limpopo could get to school, but when officials went to check there were no bridges to be found.

'There were hundreds of examples of malfeasance during that time,' says Gordhan. 'The first rot was beginning to become visible.'

When evidence of widespread corruption emerged in the Free State, Limpopo and KwaZulu-Natal, Gordhan issued these provinces with Section 100 interventions, which allows the national government to take control of provincial departments when the province has failed to fulfil, or cannot fulfil, its functions.

Gordhan had another taste of 'the rot' when Zuma summoned him to an urgent meeting in 2013. Gordhan set out the details of that meeting in the affidavit he submitted to the Zondo commission in October 2018.

Gordhan hadn't been told what the meeting was about; he'd just been informed that the president wanted to see him urgently. When he and his director-general, Lungisa Fuzile, arrived at Mahlamba Ndlopfu, Zuma wasn't there yet. Instead, they found his key energy adviser, Senti Thobejane.

'Mr Thobejane's presence was the first inkling we had that the former president wished to discuss nuclear procurement with us that day. Mr Thobejane explained the technical details of the procurement of nuclear power generation capacity to Mr Fuzile and me. I asked him who the major players were in the field, and he explained that the United States, France, China, South Korea and Russia were all possible suppliers of the technology to South Africa.'

Gordhan was struck by the fact that the then minister of energy, Ben Martins, and the then director-general of the department of energy, Nelisiwe Magubane, weren't present at the meeting.

'Eventually, the former president arrived and joined us. I explained to him that we'd been talking to Mr Thobejane for some time, and that he had been explaining the nuclear technology and its possible suppliers to us. Mr Zuma indicated that South Africa needed nuclear power and that a process should be initiated to procure it.'

Gordhan told Zuma that nuclear procurement was a complex issue, and that there were lots of interested stakeholders, such as various competing suppliers and environmentalists. He indicated that the treasury could undertake an exercise to design a procurement process for such a significant project, and to ensure that it complied with the applicable legal framework for public and energy procurement.

'I made this undertaking after I indicated to the former president that it would be appropriate to follow lawful procurement procedures for such an expensive project to avoid becoming mired in scandal like the so-called arms deal. I wanted to impress upon the former president that undertaking the nuclear procurement required careful consideration of its costs, the choice of supplier, due process, and the likely challenges to any decision to proceed.'

A short while after that meeting, an official at the treasury received a call from someone in government who wanted advice about a clause on a tax issue in a contract that South Africa was about to sign with Russia. When the official probed, he found out it was the nuclear deal.

'You don't have to know anything about nuclear to know that there are lots of people who are sceptical of it – and not only greenie activists,' says the treasury official. 'I mean, who thinks they can quietly sign a deal with Russia? It's wrong.'

As Gordhan detailed in his affidavit to the Zondo commission, 'The so-called nuclear deal first came to the attention of officials at the National Treasury at some point in 2013 when a draft cooperation agreement, to be signed with Russia, was provided because it included a tax-incentive structure. The Department of Energy approached [the] National Treasury for input on this incentive structure, and to consider and assess the implications under the Public Finance Management Act. Officials within [the] National Treasury raised concerns with this draft agreement and its clear objective of creating firm fiscal commitments to Russia by South Africa.'

In his affidavit, Gordhan stated that the level of personal interest shown by Zuma in the 'nuclear deal' was 'an early manifestation of the profound interest that the former President had in what should have been ordinary transactional matters subject to due diligence, affordability and feasibility studies'.

The price tag for the 9.6GW of nuclear-power-generating capacity that Zuma wanted South Africa to buy from Russia? More than R1 trillion.

A senior government colleague says the country owes Gordhan a debt of gratitude for not signing off on the nuclear deal when Zuma tried to push it through in that 'urgent' meeting he'd called. 'Pravin had to play the game. If he'd just said no, he would've been fired, and then someone more compliant would've been brought in and the project would [have gone] ahead. But Pravin insisted that nuclear go through a proper process and for there to be a feasibility study.

Pravin Gordhan was born in a country in which he couldn't go to certain places because of the colour of his skin – but the young PG (at 10, left, and above with friends at around the same age) thought that was just the way things were.

It was only when Gordhan (front row, far left) went to Sastri College, an Indian boys' high school in Durban, that he started to realise that racism was an issue.

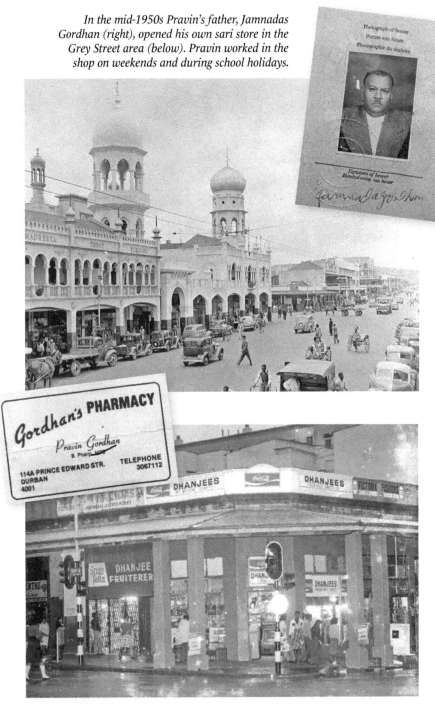

In the mid-1950s Pravin's father, Jamnadas Gordhan (right), opened his own sari store in the Grey Street area (below). Pravin worked in the shop on weekends and during school holidays.

Gordhan's PHARMACY

Pravin Gordhan
B. Pharm. MPS

114A PRINCE EDWARD STR.
DURBAN
4001

TELEPHONE
3067112

Activists would congregate in shops such as this one on the corner of Grey and Victoria streets. When Gordhan was fired from King Edward VIII Hospital in the early 1980s, he set up his own pharmacy, which similarly became a meeting place for activists.

Campaign grows to get ex-detainee's job back

A CAMPAIGN demanding the reinstatement of ex-detainee, Pravin Gordhan, to his job at Durban's King Edward VIII hospital is rapidly gaining momentum.

Gordhan was dismissed while still in detention. A qualified pharmacist, he was employed at King Edward VIII Hospital from 1974 until his dismissal on December 21 1981.

He was detained on November 27 1981. On May 7 he was released with a 2-year banning order and placed under house arrest. At the time of his dismissal he was told he would in all likelihood get his job back on his release but his application was turned down.

In his eight years at the hospital, Gordhan was never reprimanded for neglecting his duties, nor was any

Pravin Gordhan

mention ever made of "low productivity" or "continued absenteeism". Yet these were some of the reasons for dismissal cited by officials of the Natal Provincial Administration (NPA).

The provincial authorities have also claimed there "is no suitable post" to which he can be appointed despite the fact that numerous posts for pharmacists at Durban's provincial hospitals have recently been advertised.

Gordhan has been offered jobs at private pharmacies outside the Durban magisterial district. He has applied to the authorities for modification of his banning order to be made to enable him to take up employment. This too has been refused.

Spearheading the campaign for Gordhan's reinstatement, is the Natal Health Workers' Association (NHWA) of which he is a member, in conjunction with the Medical Graduates Association, the Medical Students Representative Council of the University of Natal and the Alternate Medical Association.

Gordhan (above, far left) peers at documents held by Thumba Pillay, then an attorney and now a judge, after he and others were arrested in 1981. Also in the picture are activists Kreesan Naicker (centre back, in the white shirt), Fatima Meer (bottom right), Swami Gounden (between Naicker and Meer) and Dhaya Pillay (in front of Gounden), who's now a judge.

The October 1982 edition of the Saspu National *(above) reported on efforts to get Gordhan his job back after King Edward VIII Hospital fired him while he was in detention. In 1990 Gordhan and several other Operation Vula operatives were arrested and charged; the following year, they were granted indemnity, as reported by the* Sunday Times *(right and below).*

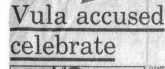

Vula accused celebrate

CLEARED: (clockwise) ANC members Pravin Gordhan, Deepak Patel, Billy Nair and Aniesh Sankar are four of the nine Operation Vula accused granted indemnity by the government on Friday. The alleged plot by the ANC and Communist Party's underground wing that was revealed by police in a blaze of publicity last year at times threatened talks between the ANC and the government. After spending several months in detention, the nine were granted bail.

Picture: MS ROY

OPERATION VULA ACCUSED ... (from left standing) Amnesh Sankar, Pravin Gordhan, Susenna Tshabalala, Raymond Lala, Dipak Patel, (seated) Catherine Mvelase, Billy Nair, Siphiwe Nyanda and Mac Maharaj. Picture: JIMMY HUTT

Accused don't look like characters out of spy nove

Pravin and Vani Gordhan meet Nelson Mandela and Graça Machel.

Pravin Gordhan in the 1990s (left) and now.

Gordhan (far right) with Diakonia ecumenical centre founder and human-rights activist Paddy Kearney (far left) and former KwaZulu-Natal premier Willies Mchunu.

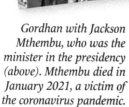

Gordhan with Jackson Mthembu, who was the minister in the presidency (above). Mthembu died in January 2021, a victim of the coronavirus pandemic.

Finance minister Gordhan and his deputy Mcebisi Jonas (above).

Gordhan with legendary activists Swami Gounden (seated) and Sunny and Urmila Singh (centre back).

By order of His Excellency, The President, I have been directed to communicate an urgent message to your good selves that the permission for you to travel to the UK and the USA from 26 to 31 March 2017 has been been rescinded with immediate effect. In that regard, His Excellency has directed that I request your good selves to return to the Republic of South Africa, as soon as you receive this message. Further, His Excellency has directed that you instruct DG Lungisa Fuzile to accompany your good selves back home. His Excellency The President will be dispatching a formal directive to your respective offices tomorrow morning, 27 March 2017.

With my best wishes

Yours sincerely

(Signed)
R. Cassius Lubisi, PhD

Pravin Gordhan and Jacob Zuma – who share a birthday and home province – were once comrades. The 'recall' message (left) sent to Gordhan on Zuma's behalf in March 2017 culminated in him being fired as finance minister. Supporters gathered outside the treasury in Pretoria to show their support for Gordhan (below, saluting the gathering).

Gordhan (front row, third from left) at the April 2017 memorial service for Ahmed Kathrada where he made his 'connect the dots' speech (right).

Pravin and Vani Gordhan

'People like to shout, "Cut government bureaucracy," but there's good bureaucracy and there's bad bureaucracy. Without that good bureaucracy, the country would be sitting with a crippling nuclear project today. Pravin played a sterling role in making sure the proposed nuclear project went through a proper process.'

When Zuma couldn't get his way, he bypassed the treasury and fired people who stood in his way and replaced them with compliant toadies.

❖

On 7 May 2014 South Africans went to the polls to vote in the country's fifth democratic election – and once again they returned the ANC to power.

After Jacob Zuma's inauguration ceremony on 24 May, Gordhan's cellphone rang and once again it was Gwede Mantashe, who told him that the president wanted an audience with him. And, like five years earlier, Gordhan made his way to Mahlamba Ndlopfu to wait his turn to see Zuma. However, this time when he was called in, he was told that he was being deployed to the cooperative governance and traditional affairs (CoGTA) portfolio because of his familiarity with local-government matters – Gordhan had chaired the portfolio committee on local government when he was a member of parliament (MP) from 1994 to 1999 – and to prepare for the local-government elections in 2016.

As Hogan had found out, if you stood in Zuma's way, you were 'redeployed'.

❖

Removing Gordhan had had little to do with his performance as a finance minister. The markets had liked Manuel, and had seen

Gordhan as a continuity figure when he was appointed in 2009. 'Pravin was seen as a safe pair of hands,' says Jonathan Rosenthal, *The Economist*'s Africa editor. 'He had run a tight ship at SARS, which [had] allowed Manuel to reduce taxes, increase spending and bring down the deficit all at the same time, and because of that, South Africa went into the financial crisis in a very strong position. This meant Gordhan had the fiscal space to give an economic boost to try to cushion the blow.'

Goolam Ballim, chief economist and head of research for the Standard Bank Group, refers to two themes in Gordhan's tenure as finance minister: sustainability and tradeoffs.

Sustainability, he explains, hinges on the finance minister's ability to enduringly maintain sound financial management – accumulate revenues, manage expenditure and simultaneously contain debt service payments. Tradeoffs, Ballim says, go to the heart of economics and are an attempt to balance any country's 'unlimited wants with its limited resources'.

'In a country such as ours, given the enormity of [the] deliberate deprivation during apartheid, it was inevitable that South Africa would endure a multi-decade episode of attempting to recalibrate for a more equal society, to lower poverty and to buoy employment and social welfare.'

Although Ballim says the true success of a finance minister might only be recognised years or even decades later, he believes Gordhan understood and implemented those fundamentals. 'Minister Gordhan appreciated that sustainability is an inherently long-term concept, and he allocated public finances where [they were] likely to boost growth ... He also had the courage to make incredibly hard tradeoffs with a long-term view in mind.'

Ballim adds that there won't be a consensus of opinion in appraising Gordhan's performance. He believes he's likely to receive a glowing tribute from the finance sector, while the union movement's assessment would probably be less than favourable.

Financial journalist Ann Crotty points out that Gordhan was responsible for signing off on the public-sector wage agreement that resulted in public-sector wages bloating over the past ten years. 'The ballooning public-sector wage bill was a major factor in government debt getting out of control, from the very controlled levels under Manuel,' she says.

While comparisons between Gordhan and Manuel are perhaps inevitable, they're not particularly useful. Gordhan didn't have the sort of support from Zuma that Trevor Manuel had from Thabo Mbeki; and, of course, Gordhan had to contend with the tough international financial situation that prevailed during his stint as finance minister, whereas Manuel had a very benign international setting.

Gordhan also had to contend with a diminishing level of expertise. At the start of his term, a number of highly skilled people in key positions who were worried about Zuma's presidency resigned to go into the private sector to protect their futures.

Despite these setbacks, it's widely agreed that Gordhan was getting on top of his portfolio, and that removing him didn't make sense – especially if you consider that the rotation of ministers creates turmoil. Each time a new minister comes in, he or she has to get on top of the role, get up to speed with the details and understand what the objectives are.

But Gordhan had become an obstacle, and he wasn't surprised when he was shunted aside. There'd been speculation in political and media circles that he was going to be removed as finance minister.

'So,' says Gordhan, 'your question, why did Zuma originally choose me as finance minister in 2009? He probably had his own calculations … but then realised that he couldn't quite manipulate me.'

The person Zuma appointed to replace Gordhan as minister of

finance was Nhlanhla Nene. Zuma clearly thought Nene might be more willing to be persuaded to do his bidding.

But Nene was made of sterner stuff. Zuma had once again picked the wrong man.

10
Fired

As minister of cooperative governance and traditional affairs, the political heat was off Pravin Gordhan. He rolled up his sleeves and got stuck into his new portfolio.

CoGTA's role is to ensure the three spheres of government – local, provincial and national – work together efficiently to deliver essential services to communities. When Gordhan took his chair at CoGTA, at least a third of South Africa's municipalities had become dysfunctional. There were more and more service-delivery protests taking place and they were becoming increasingly violent.

Mcebisi Jonas, who was deputy minister of finance when Gordhan was at CoGTA, worked with Gordhan to help sort out 'the mess at local government'. 'Many municipalities had lost touch with their functions: supplying water, water reticulation, cleaning, and ensuring the rubbish bins were collected ... you know, basic services,' says Jonas.

Unlike the steep learning curves that came with his appointments to SARS and as finance minister, CoGTA was familiar territory for Gordhan. He'd come from a civic background and he continued to live by the 'higher purpose' mantra. Within no time he'd understood the situation at local government and had developed a back-to-basics campaign.

Gordhan started to intervene in poorly performing municipalities that didn't keep records of their transactions, that employed people who weren't fit for purpose, and whose officials wasted taxpayers' money by paying expensive consultants to do their work for them. He warned public servants that there would be serious consequences for corruption, and he opened up procurement processes to public oversight, providing transparency and accountability to keep 'all of us honest'.

He said CoGTA's motto should be 'No service failures', and where there was one, services should be restored urgently.

Gordhan realised that municipalities had lost touch with not only delivering basic services but also the other basic functions, such as collecting revenue from citizens and allocating it in a strategic way.

'The conversation between [the] treasury and CoGTA improved in that period, because of this thinking,' says Jonas. 'We worked a lot to understand municipal finance and how to support the goals of taking municipalities back to their core business.'

Gordhan's initiatives at CoGTA were starting to take root and he was enjoying his new and relatively stress-free role when South Africa was rocked by 9/12 – 'Nenegate'.

On 9 December 2015, a cabinet meeting approved South Africa's nuclear-procurement programme, although finance minister Nhlanhla Nene reiterated that he wouldn't sign off on the deal if the country couldn't afford it. An hour after the cabinet meeting, President Jacob Zuma summoned Nene to his office. The meeting between the two men lasted two or three minutes, but its impact was still felt many years down the line.

In those few minutes Zuma fired Nene, a move that sent South Africa's economy to the edge of a fiscal precipice.

Nene walked out of the meeting, took out his cellphone and typed a message to Jonas, his deputy. 'The axe has fallen,' he wrote.

Trevor Manuel, the minister of finance from 1996 to 2009 and minister in the presidency responsible for the national planning commission in Zuma's cabinet, was gobsmacked when he heard Nene had been fired. He couldn't understand why the president would, without reason, drop a decent, hardworking, committed, smart, efficient and capable minister like Nene.

But there *was* a reason. A trillion-rand reason.

'People can say what they want about the firing of Nene,' says Jonas, 'but I still genuinely believe it had to do with the nuclear deal. I hear many theories but as a person who was there, I can tell you now that the big issue was the nuclear deal. It was actually the biggest issue. It triggered Nene's firing.'

'I believe that I was removed from office because of my refusal to toe the line in relation to certain projects,' Nene told the Zondo commission on 3 October 2018. The other project he was referring to related to a clash with Dudu Myeni, a Zuma confidante who headed up the Friends of Jacob Zuma Foundation and was the chairperson of the bankrupt South African Airways (SAA). Myeni had been pushing for the purchase of ten aircraft, which Nene had resisted.

At 8pm, just two hours after Nene had been unceremoniously dumped, Zuma named a parliamentary backbencher – someone who sits in parliament but doesn't hold office in the government – as his replacement. The new finance minister was such an unknown entity that no one was sure what his first name was. Official releases referred to him variously as Desmond, Douglas and David.

The person Zuma had plucked from obscurity was Des van Rooyen, a former mayor of Merafong local municipality in Gauteng. It later emerged that Van Rooyen had met with the Gupta brothers several times shortly before his contentious appointment. It seems he was a man who had the endorsement of the Gupta brothers.

Ajay, Atul and Rajesh Gupta had arrived in South Africa from India in the 1990s and quickly established themselves as influential businessmen. They met Jacob Zuma in 2002 and cultivated a relationship with him. When Zuma became president seven years later, they allegedly used their access to him to wrangle all manner of government contracts and redirect billions of rands of public funds to their companies.

The depth of the Zuma-Gupta relationship and the enormous power the brothers wielded over the president became evident in April 2013 when a chartered jet ferrying two hundred guests from India to an opulent Gupta family wedding at Sun City bypassed immigration and landed at the military airport, Waterkloof Air Force Base, outside Pretoria. The instruction to allow the unauthorised landing had come from 'Number One'.

Goolam Aboobaker had been in Gordhan's office when 'a very fancy invitation' to the Gupta wedding arrived for him. 'Pravin made it clear that he was not even going to respond to it. By then he felt the Guptas had compromised Zuma in some significant way,' says Aboobaker.

The Guptas controlled the Shiva uranium mine and, with uranium being the fuel most widely used by nuclear plants, they would have made an untold fortune if the trillion-rand nuclear deal with Russia had gone through. It was seemingly the Guptas, who already had their hands on the levers of SOEs, who were pushing the nuclear buttons in their quest to amass vast wealth for themselves.

So when Nene, and Gordhan before him, proved to be hurdles to the deal that Zuma wanted to strike with Russian president Vladimir Putin, he got rid of them and appointed Van Rooyen, who was seen as a Gupta-friendly minister.

Nene had earned high praise during his eighteen months as

finance minister, and the market response to his firing was swift and blunt, which seemed to take Zuma by surprise. The price of bonds fell sharply, billions were wiped off the stock exchange and the rand went into free fall, plummeting within days from about R13 to the dollar to around R16 to the dollar.

In her testimony to the Zondo commission in February 2019, national treasury economist Catherine MacLeod explained that investors were concerned that a change of finance minister would weaken the treasury and its ability to block unsustainable projects like the nuclear build. She said that a change in finance ministers would usually not have resulted in a negative reaction by the market, but that 'Nenegate' had been different because of the way in which it had been executed, and that Van Rooyen was perceived as a risk to investors.

Gordhan told the Zondo commission that the 'devastating impact of this unexpected announcement on the South African economy is estimated to be approximately R500 billion'.

The political fallout was as fast and as severe. Civil-society activists, religious bodies, academics and trade unionists united in their criticism of Zuma. Public servants in the treasury threatened to quit. Former health minister Barbara Hogan called on Zuma to resign, saying he'd crossed a line and needed to be held to account. Organised business groups and high-profile ANC members met with Zuma, urging him to reconsider Van Rooyen's appointment.

But Zuma appeared unmoved. Speaking at an ANC rally on the Sunday morning, four days after his cabinet reshuffle, he said that criticism about Van Rooyen's appointment came from 'people who talk a lot on TV'.

However, something – or someone – managed to move the then president, because later that afternoon Pravin Gordhan received a message from Lakela Kaunda, the chief operations officer in the presidency, saying Zuma wanted to meet with him. Moments later Jessie Duarte, the ANC deputy secretary-general, called Gordhan and told him that Zuma was going to ask him to do something and that he should not refuse the request. He received a similar message from Cyril Ramaphosa, then the country's deputy president.

◆

Gordhan made his way to the presidential home, Mahlamba Ndlopfu, and listened as Zuma told him that although he believed Des van Rooyen was perfectly suitable as finance minister, he wanted Gordhan to take up the position in order to calm the markets.

At first Gordhan resisted. 'There are other people,' he told Zuma. 'I'm enjoying CoGTA.'

But Zuma pressed him. Gordhan told the president he needed to call his wife and discuss this development with her.

After putting down the phone, he told Zuma that he would accept the position, but that he had conditions. He wanted several issues resolved as soon as possible: the ongoing dire financial predicament of SAA and specifically the role of Dudu Myeni in it; the proposed nuclear-procurement deal; and Tom Moyane's role as SARS commissioner.

Zuma agreed, and the keys to the treasury were taken away from Van Rooyen, whose four-day stint as finance minister came to an abrupt end, earning him the nickname 'Weekend Special', the title of Afropop musician Brenda Fassie's hit song.

Gordhan's return resulted in the markets stabilising quite quickly, because the economy had been returned to a safe pair of hands. Zuma, however, was already plotting how he could get rid of Gordhan.

People close to Gordhan say that from the very first day of his reappointment as finance minister, Zuma and all the ministers who supported him launched open attacks on Gordhan. 'Everything was blocked. PG was under siege,' says a senior treasury official.

Gordhan thinks about it. 'Perhaps "siege" isn't quite the right word,' he says, 'but, yes, the gloves had come off and I was under huge attack. But, you know, it was nothing that couldn't be managed.'

The following day, Gordhan held a press conference at which he said he wouldn't be deviating from Nene's path. He also accused some officials of treating state enterprises 'as if [they're] a personal toy from which you can extract money when you feel like it'.

At his side was Mcebisi Jonas, Nene's former number two, who had somehow kept his position as deputy finance minister despite showing that he wasn't prepared to be a Gupta stooge. Two months before Nene's axing, Jonas had allegedly been offered (and rejected) a R600-million bribe by Ajay Gupta, to be the minister of finance. Duduzane Zuma, the president's son and a Gupta business partner, had been at that meeting.

'That first press conference with PG was tense,' recalls Jonas. On the duo's to-do list was how they would manage the twin controversies of the nuclear deal and SAA, how they would generate economic growth, and their plans to manage the fiscus to ensure there was a strategic deployment of resources, and at the same time manage expenditure. 'We had to explain what the new direction on all of those issues was.'

The journalists wanted to know what the plan was with the nuclear deal. 'PG was robust and our stance on nuclear was nuanced, but people could read between the lines that we were saying no to it. The position we articulated was that we weren't inherently opposed to it, but that if we got into nuclear, it would be done in a manner and scale consistent with our fiscal capacity. If you read that very well, it meant the nuclear deal wouldn't happen.

'At the end of that press conference I joked to PG and said, "Hey, we'll be fired. It's not a matter of if, it's a matter of when."'

Jonas says that what followed was an intense period of tension between the treasury and the presidency. 'It was a continuation of the Nene era ... Of course, there were other issues, and there will always be issues between [the] treasury and [the] presidency, but the main issue was the nuclear one.'

Two months after losing their finance minister, the Guptas experienced a second setback. Absa bank had conducted a risk assessment of the controversial family and decided to cut banking ties with the Gupta company Oakbay.

On 19 February 2016, as Gordhan was putting the final touches to his budget speech for that year, an envelope was hand-delivered to the treasury. It contained 27 questions from the police's elite crime-investigation unit, the Hawks, relating to the SARS high-risk investigations unit, or, as the *Sunday Times* insisted on calling it, the 'SARS rogue unit'. The Hawks gave Gordhan two weeks to answer the questions.

Was it just a coincidence that the questions had arrived so soon after Gordhan's appointment had been imposed on Zuma?

When Gordhan got the 27 questions he went straight to Zuma. 'I handed him the questions and asked, "What is this all about?" He doesn't like confrontation, and I told him to his face that we'd survived the oppression of the security police in the apartheid era only to [have to be prepared] to be eliminated under democracy. He was just flipping the pages of the 27 questions, not reading them, just flipping the pages. "Oh, I'll check." That was all he said. "I'll check."'

Two months later, the media reported that the Hawks were investigating charges against Gordhan in relation to the SARS unit, and for approving the early retirement of former SARS boss Ivan Pillay and then rehiring him as a consultant. The Hawks asked Gordhan to go to their office to make a 'warning statement', sparking speculation that Gordhan was about to be arrested.

In the meantime, South Africa's three other big banks – First National Bank, Nedbank and Standard Bank – had joined Absa in cutting ties with the Guptas. Following the banks' announcement, the country's Financial Intelligence Centre, which was established in 2001 to identify the proceeds of crime and combat money laundering, among other tasks, listed 72 apparently suspicious transactions totalling almost R7 billion, implicating the Guptas and their companies.

Oakbay's CEO Nazeem Howa asked Gordhan to get the banks to reverse their decision, but Gordhan told him it would be unlawful and improper for him to intervene in a private contractual relationship between a bank and its client.

Mineral resources minister Mosebenzi Zwane, whose relationship with the Guptas would later feature before the Zondo commission, tried to bully the banks in an attempt to force them to change their minds. According to Gordhan, Zwane had Zuma's full backing and support in undermining and maligning Gordhan's stance in relation to the closure of the bank accounts. When Gordhan announced that he had no authority to intervene, Zwane threatened to take away the banks' operating licences.

Zuma then announced the appointment of a ministerial task team consisting of Zwane, Gordhan and labour minister Mildred Oliphant, to probe the closing of Gupta accounts. Gordhan wasn't at the cabinet meeting at which the team was formed, and declined to participate. His concerns that members of the executive shouldn't interfere in contractual relationships between banks and their customers were ignored.

Giving evidence at the Zondo commission in September 2018, Standard Bank's Ian Sinton said the bank had been summoned to a meeting with ANC heavyweights Gwede Mantashe, Jessie Duarte and

Enoch Godongwana at the party's Luthuli House headquarters. 'We were asked to comment on perceptions that we were part of white monopoly capital oppressing black businesses, and that we were taking instructions from Stellenbosch to close accounts,' Sinton said.

'White monopoly capital' was a phrase employed by the Guptas' public-relations agency, British experts Bell Pottinger, which employed a strategy of diverting attention from media coverage critical of the Guptas by pointing fingers at 'white capital' and its 'poster boy', Johann Rupert, chair of Stellenbosch-based Remgro and one of the country's richest men.

'I must say it was the first time I saw my boss, Sim Tshabalala [chief executive of the Standard Bank Group], get really angry,' Sinton added.

After the Guptas repeatedly pressured Gordhan to intervene to have their accounts reopened, the minister decided to ask the high court for a declaratory order confirming he couldn't get involved in the dispute between Oakbay and the banks. Gordhan lost this application, not because the court found that the finance minister did have the authority to intervene, but because the law already existed stating that he didn't – so a declaratory order wouldn't be necessary.

And still the attacks continued. Two weeks before Gordhan was to deliver his mid-term budget speech in October 2016, the controversial national director of public prosecutions Shaun Abrahams announced that fraud charges were to be brought against Gordhan, former SARS commissioner Oupa Magashula and Pillay.

At the time, Gordhan was on an international roadshow to drum up investor support. *The Economist*'s Jonathan Rosenthal had secured an interview with him in London and remembers that, despite the rumours of his possible arrest, Gordhan was upbeat. 'We chatted and it was clear that Pravin was here to sell South Africa. He stayed on message even though he was under all this political pressure. At the end of the interview I wished him luck and said it must be quite frightening to be going back and possibly being arrested. He looked at me and, with absolute calmness, said, "Jonathan, I've been through much worse. I've been arrested, I've been tortured. This is nothing. There's nothing that they can do to frighten me." I thought, *This is one courageous man.*

However, Abrahams made an abrupt about-turn a few days later and withdrew the charges.

Still, the attempts to dislodge Gordhan continued. As he explained to the Zondo commission, 'It was a year of ongoing harassment and attempted destruction of me by law-enforcement agencies, some media houses, and a persistent social-media campaign of fake news and personal attacks that appeared antagonistic towards me and the work being done by [the] Treasury. I was the target of an orchestrated campaign that appeared aimed at forcing me to resign as Minister of Finance.'

'He was being battered from every side,' says one of Gordhan's former advisers, who added that the onslaught caused Gordhan's health to suffer.

Judge Dennis Davis, who'd become friendly with Gordhan during the Codesa days, says the attack on Gordhan took a terrible toll. 'I was there when Shaun the Sheep [as Abrahams became known, as he was seen as a Zuma yes-man] was issuing various barbs. The pressure was extraordinary but Pravin has incredible resilience to deal with these things. Zuma and his cronies totally underestimated the level of tenacity and fortitude that he has.'

'Of course it was tough,' says Gordhan. 'It was very tough, but not impossible to cope with. I had so many signals sent to me which said please don't leave. So, like the fool that I am, instead of just getting out of the way and retiring, I stuck around and I basically acted as a punching bag for these people, and took the punches, because the higher purpose was still to be served in that the treasury mustn't be handed over to these guys.'

He adds that he owes a lot to his own family, who also took a battering. 'A normal family would've said, "Hey, leave … or else." I'm very privileged to have a former activist as my wife, so she understands and is equally passionate about justice, and things being done in the right kind of way.'

Jonas described that year as 'probably the most intense period in the post-apartheid history of South Africa'.

Derek Hanekom, who was minister of tourism in the Zuma administration, and who became politically close to Gordhan during this time, says, 'We were starting to find out more about the role of the Guptas as it was unfolding, and there was a growing realisation that we were up against quite evil forces. A few of us [in cabinet] were prepared to stand up to block some of the things that they were trying to do. We also knew that if we didn't get rid of Zuma, we were going to be in very deep trouble.'

Hanekom began to mobilise fellow members of the ANC's NEC to urge Zuma to step down. 'I was the frontline person – a bit by accident, but that's how it works – to call on him directly to step down as president of South Africa. A number of NEC members did support the call, but not enough.'

⟡

While Gordhan was fending off these attacks he had to continue doing his job. On 26 March 2017, with Zuma's approval, he boarded a plane for London to embark on a roadshow to woo potential investors. He also intended to shore up confidence with global ratings agencies, which independently evaluate and publish research on all bonds issued by corporations and governments. Gordhan was going to try to ensure that South Africa's economy didn't slide into 'junk' territory, which would signal to investors that the risk of the country's debt had increased and that the government might not have enough money to pay back what it had borrowed.

Back in South Africa, Zuma, who fancied himself as a chess hustler always a few steps ahead of his political opponents, was briefing senior ANC and SACP officials about Operation Checkmate. This, he explained, was a secret intelligence dossier that revealed that Pravin Gordhan and Mcebisi Jonas were conspiring with foreign forces to topple him from power.

Zuma is in fact an ardent player of chess, a game he learned when he was incarcerated on Robben Island – the prisoners made chess boards from thin cardboard and chess pieces from corks. In 2010, addressing a gala dinner for Moves for Life, an organisation that uses chess to promote maths and science education among poor children, and of which Zuma is patron, he explained how chess enhances your ability 'to make thoughtful, considered, strategic decisions under pressure'. He said these skills were essential for decision-making when you're entrusted with serious leadership positions.

While Pravin Gordhan was in the air, London bound, on that Sunday night in March 2017, in South Africa, Jacob Zuma was drafting a message ordering his finance minister to return home immediately.

11

A Dramatic Week

Mcebisi Jonas, who'd also received the text message to return to South Africa but who hadn't actually left the country yet at that stage, called people in the presidency to ask what was going on but no one could — or would – tell him.

He called Pravin Gordhan in London and asked him if he knew what it was all about. But Gordhan was also in the dark.

Jonas reminded Gordhan that he'd predicted at that first post-Nenegate press conference fifteen months earlier that they would be fired, and suggested that the recall meant the axe was about to fall.

'When I look back, I think it was them [the Guptas] who were in a rush to kick us out because they were trying to put in a new minister who would immediately remove the obstacles in their way so that they could continue to benefit [from mega projects],' says Jonas. 'But PG was determined to fight. He was confident. That's another feature of PG: in the most difficult situation, where your life is threatened, he shines. He is very strong and determined.'

By the time Gordhan landed back in South Africa on 28 March 2017, he knew two things: his job as finance minister was hanging by a thread, and his boss, Jacob Zuma, was scraping the bottom of the barrel.

'Pulling me out of the roadshow was emblematic of the kind of desperation that Zuma had, with pressure probably coming from the Guptas, to "get rid of this fellow", says Gordhan. 'What ultimately led to Mr Charming reaching a point of desperation was that he suddenly decided, "[Former minister of public service and administration Ngoako] Ramatlhodi has been difficult and is not cooperating with my son Duduzane and the Guptas; Hanekom has asked for my removal; this fellow has been stubborn about [the] treasury ... so let's chop [off] all these heads." That was a sign of desperation on his part.'

The front pages of the newspapers that morning had lit up with Gordhan's recall, which had seen the rand nosedive again. People wondered whether it meant South Africa was facing a cabinet reshuffle – the eleventh since Zuma had come to power in 2009.

Local radio talk shows were filled with speculation about what would happen if Gordhan, whom many South Africans viewed as a man of tremendous integrity, was fired. With evidence of state capture mounting against Zuma and the Guptas, Gordhan was widely seen as a bulwark against corruption.

Jonas recalls once asking Gordhan if he ever wondered how their battle against the corrupt forces would end. 'He told me that the very nature of these kinds of fights is that you don't have the end in sight, you're not too sure about the outcome, and we should accept that. He said we know what we would like, we know what our objective is, and we must hope we get to that point. I found this very interesting. You start down a road and you don't know where it's going to end, and you just continue because you believe in what you're doing.

'I think that's the hallmark of PG's life. He's a very optimistic person who is driven by a fundamental set of values.'

❖

Soon after he landed back in South Africa, Gordhan made his way to Luthuli House, where secretary-general Gwede Mantashe briefed him on what had happened. 'Mantashe told me Zuma had met with the ANC's Top Six officials and had waved this two page so-called intelligence report, which they kicked out.' The report, codenamed Operation Checkmate, was so amateurish that EFF leader Julius Malema later remarked that it looked like it had been written by a child.

When the other five of the ANC's most senior officials – Mantashe, deputy president Cyril Ramaphosa, national chairperson Baleka Mbete, deputy secretary-general Jessie Duarte and treasurer general Zweli Mkhize – rejected the report, Zuma tried a new tack, which was to complain of a breakdown in relations between him and Gordhan.

Gordhan shakes his head. 'Why the officials believed that rubbish is another story. This is not a normal employment relationship where you have a "breakdown in relations". And there was no indication there was a breakdown anyway – where there was a standoff or verbal exchange, whatever the case might be. It was a cooked-up story.'

Mantashe told Gordhan that Zuma would prefer it if he resigned, rather than the president having to fire him. '[Mantashe] spoke to me about leaving with my integrity or honour intact.'

Gordhan had no plans to do Zuma's dirty work for him, and told Mantashe that if the president wanted to get rid of him, he would have to fire him. The country was abuzz with rumours of a Gordhan-Zuma showdown.

That day, former Robben Island prisoner and icon of the struggle against apartheid Ahmed Kathrada died. Kathrada, affectionately known as 'Uncle Kathy', had been one of the last surviving leaders of the Mandela generation. He'd also become a fierce critic of Zuma, and a year earlier he'd called on Zuma to resign when the constitutional court had found the then president had violated his oath of office by refusing to comply with the public protector's remedial action, including the repayment of public money spent on renovations to his private Nkandla homestead.

In a most profound snub, the Kathrada family asked that Zuma not attend his funeral, which took place the following day.

At the funeral, senior ANC figures used the opportunity to pay tribute to Kathrada and to criticise Zuma's cronyism and corruption. Former president Kgalema Motlanthe read from a letter Kathrada had written to Zuma the previous year: 'Is it asking too much to express the hope that you will consider stepping down?'

Gordhan and his wife, Vanitha, arrived at the funeral and were making their way to the back of the venue when his comrade from the struggle days, Valli Moosa, urged them to come up to the front and sit in the second row.

Neeshan Bolton, the director of the Ahmed Kathrada Foundation, asked Gordhan to stand up, and then said that whether Gordhan remained in his post or not, he epitomised the principles for which Uncle Kathy had stood. The crowd roared their approval.

Gordhan choked back tears.

The next day, a Thursday, Gordhan and Jonas still hadn't learned their fate.

Jonas was at work as usual when a senior government official knocked on his office door and asked him to go for a walk. They ended up at a restaurant where the man blurted out, 'Hey, you and PG are both going to be fired.'

Jonas recalls: 'I said, "Really?" and asked him how he knew. He said he couldn't tell me but that he knew for a fact. I returned to the office and found PG and told him the news that we were going to be fired. We debated whether we should call a press conference and fire ourselves, but decided to rather stay on and see when it happened.'

They didn't have to wait too much longer. That night, just after midnight, Gordhan became aware of his removal when Zuma's announcement of a cabinet reshuffle was broadcast on television while he watched. He'd been replaced by Malusi Gigaba, who was linked to the Guptas. Ngoako Ramatlhodi was also out, as was tourism minister Derek Hanekom.

Hanekom wasn't surprised: he'd been actively campaigning for Zuma to step down, and when his last attempt at the ANC's NEC meeting had failed, he'd realised that the only avenue left was to make sure Zuma and his allies didn't succeed at the ANC national conference at Nasrec that December.

Jonas was at home when he received calls from people telling him to watch TV. He switched on his set and learned that he and Gordhan had been fired. 'Zuma never spoke to us about firing us, by the way,' says Jonas. 'There was no phone call, no message. I've always wondered why he didn't tell us he was firing us. I'm sure it was because he knew fundamentally that it was wrong. He knew that decision was being taken for nefarious reasons.'

Jonas recalls Gordhan phoning him in the morning. 'PG said, "Hey, boet, did you watch this thing?" I said, "Ja." He said we should go to the office and say goodbye to everyone. When we got to the office the staff gave us a hero's welcome. It was very emotional.'

Gordhan remembers bringing all the staff together and telling them, 'Well, we have to go but we will continue to do what we have to do.'

They then held a press conference where it was the journalists' turn to clap and cheer – unprecedented behaviour at a political news conference. Gordhan told them that he and Jonas had joined the struggle when they were young to help bring about freedom. 'What sickens me is the allegations that I had secret meetings to undermine this country ... Let me say, categorically, there was no such meeting. Why would we do that?'

'South Africans should wake up and smell the coffee,' Jonas told the gathered journalists.

In the meantime, outside the treasury in Church Square, people had started to gather in protest as calls were made on social media to #OccupyTreasury. '[This] is not a cabinet reshuffle,' social justice activist Mark Heywood of the protest movement Save South Africa said at the time. 'It is a coup. That is the best term for it. The president has abused his legal powers to appoint to the cabinet not people who are going to serve the interests of South Africa but people who are going to serve his interests to gain control over the finances, over the banks of this country.'

Gordhan recalls, 'As we were having the press conference, the protesters walked in. It was an emotional time but we were buoyed by the very strong support for what we were trying to do.'

A memorial for Kathrada at the Johannesburg City Hall on the Saturday was packed with people of all ages, races and political affiliations. South Africans across the country with opposing ideologies and irreconcilable politics were united by a sense that something had to give ... and that something was Zuma. He'd finally gone too far.

Barbara Hogan, Kathrada's widow, who'd been an early victim of Zuma's guillotine, reiterated her call for Zuma to step down. 'You have sacrificed everything we have stood for on the altar of corruption, greed and more greed,' she said.

◈

On Thursday 6 April, a week after he'd been fired, Gordhan arrived at the memorial service for Kathrada at St George's Cathedral in

Cape Town. People cheered, ululated and sang when he entered the church.

'We have handed the state over to a bunch of gangsters,' he said to the crowd, many of whom carried posters with the slogan 'Zuma Must Fall'. 'Practising democracy is different from preaching democracy. Practising democracy means that in every situation one finds oneself, one remembers the democratic values of consultation, of listening to different views and tolerating different views even if we do disagree. Democracy also means respecting our constitution and the goals we have set in our constitution to create a democratic, non-racial, non-sexist South Africa.'

When the presidency 'postponed indefinitely' the official state memorial for Kathrada, the Nelson Mandela Foundation and the Ahmed Kathrada Foundation convened a service at the Johannesburg City Hall where, according to *Daily Maverick* journalist Richard Poplak, 'the moment belonged to Pravin Gordhan, and he seemed determined to grasp it'. 'He teared up often during the speeches, and the crowd went nuts as he made his way to the stage,' wrote Poplak. 'He seemed resolute and composed, but occasionally radiated what I'll gently describe as murderous anger.'

Gordhan, according to Poplak, gave the speech of his life. 'This propaganda channel last night said I am encouraging mass mobilisation,' Gordhan said to the crowd, referring to a bulletin on the Gupta-owned TV channel ANN7 that stated Gordhan was on a drive to encourage mass mobilisation against Zuma's government. 'Yes, I am unashamedly encouraging mass mobilisation. We are encouraging mass mobilisation to ensure that the people shall govern. This ANC is still our ANC. Uncle Kathy leaves us at a time when the problems are very clear, and who is the problem and what is the problem is very clear ...'

And then he issued a challenge to South Africans that to truly understand what was happening in the country and to see who was benefiting from state capture and where the money was going, they should 'connect the dots'.

12

Going Rogue

Launches at the quirky Johannesburg bookstore Love Books are pleasant affairs. They're a time for a writer who's spent years – sometimes decades – sweating over a manuscript to be celebrated. After some cheese and wine, the authors talk about their process and an appreciative audience nod enthusiastically, ask polite questions, and leave with a new book under their arm.

But on 20 September 2018, Love Books turned into a site of anger and protest when members of the audience turned on that night's author, Stephan Hofstatter. Hofstatter, a member of the *Sunday Times*'s erstwhile crack investigative unit, was launching *Licence to Loot: How the Plunder of Eskom and Other Parastatals Almost Sank South Africa*.

Hofstatter looked on defiantly as protesters from a group called Johannesburg Against Injustice took up their positions. They held up placards that read 'Where's the brothel?' and 'Hofstatter is a Tom Moyane stooge'. Hofstatter took photos of them.

There was an air of tense expectation as the launch got under way and the crowd waited to see what was going to happen next. When it came time for the question-and-answer session, a bald man with a grey bokkie beard got up from his chair at the back of the audience. Hofstatter's heart must have sunk when he saw who it was: Peter Richer, a former MK operative and SARS executive who'd been one of the targets in the now thoroughly discredited *Sunday Times* rolling 'rogue unit' series of articles.

Richer pointed at the author. 'I lost my job because of Stephan Hofstatter,' he began. His voice was steady but contained more than a hint of anger. He told the audience that state capture required that 'you ... get rid of ethical, hardworking, conscientious public servants'. 'And in order to do that, you set up scurrilous unethical journalists – like this one – who write stories that create the basis for those public servants to get pushed out. And we have many examples of it, all coming from a little clique in the *Sunday Times*.'

In a six-minute speech, Richer neatly summed up the saga, explaining how stories were 'concocted' about the 'so-called rogue unit'. This in turn led to the 'entire leadership of SARS [getting] pushed out'. The modus operandi ultimately gave the corrupt the freedom to loot at will. 'It happened at SARS, at the Hawks, at IPID [the Independent Police Investigative Directorate, responsible for investigating complaints against the South African Police Service and municipal police services] and at the police,' he said. He accused Hofstatter and his colleagues at the paper of being stooges of state capture and destroying people's lives, careers and reputations.

Hofstatter seemed to shrink with each rebuke.

'I'm a risk specialist. Do you think anyone is going to employ me when they look up my name and find those stories attached to my name?' asked Richer, then answered his own question: 'Not a chance.'

'We made mistakes,' Hofstatter conceded.

'That's an understatement,' one of the protesters shouted.

Hofstatter said he'd been a journalist dedicated to exposing corruption and 'never saw myself ... wanting to cause harm'.

Johann van Loggerenberg was another SARS executive who'd been hounded out of his job. Afterwards, Van Loggerenberg had contacted and eventually met with some members of the *Sunday Times* investigative unit. 'The rules with these journos were always that they didn't want it to be publicly known' that they were engaging with him, he says, but 'one of the things that I did come to learn was the manner in which the information was planted with them. I'll give you one example.

'The one journalist told me of how he would get a phone call late on a Friday. Now, their deadlines are on Saturdays ... so late on a Friday, he would get a message via a phone call to his cellphone, and it would be from a private number, which means you can't see who's calling. He would speak to somebody who he didn't know from a bar of soap. It was just a male voice, telling him to get on the Gautrain and travel from Joburg towards Tshwane, get off at the Rosebank platform, and just stand there.

'And then he would stand there and the next thing somebody would walk up to him ... hand him an envelope, walk away, and then he would get in the train, he'd go back to the office, open it up. And then they'd start writing this story.'

Other than being able to identify the source's gender and race, the *Sunday Times* investigative-unit member in question could not provide any clues to his or her identity.

Van Loggerenberg says the newspaper's 'investigative unit' did no investigating: 'If they'd done investigations, they would have sat with me and disproven what I put to them, but they just took stuff and printed it, put it into words.'

Ivan Pillay was another SARS executive who was implicated in the 'rogue unit' stories and then forced out of the organisation. He says journalists and others were fed 'something like fifteen dossiers' about SARS from 2005. 'They would go to politicians, even to the president; they would go to newspapers. And every time they came out [in print], [SARS spokesman] Adrian [Lackay] would get the operational people to work out what our response would be, [and] we would engage the journalists. And it almost always worked ... until the *Sunday Times*.'

Pillay bangs his hand on the table. 'When [the story] broke, it was unrelenting. It was week after week ... for something like 38 articles. You'd get a call, if you were lucky on a Friday, but if not, on a Saturday, and [then] you had just a few hours to respond. Later on, when we were suspended, we couldn't say anything because we were gagged by SARS regulations.'

In late 2015 and early 2016 the press ombudsman issued a series of rulings against the *Sunday Times* for its 'rogue unit' stories, ordering it to apologise to Gordhan, Pillay and Van Loggerenberg for inaccurate, misleading and unfair reportage.

On 3 April 2016, the newspaper issued what Anton Harber describes in his 2020 book *So, For The Record: Behind the Headlines in an Era of State Capture* – which is largely about the *Sunday Times* investigative unit's missteps – as an 'important' but 'incomplete' climb-down.

On 14 October 2018, after issues around the story had bubbled up again, the *Sunday Times* finally apologised unconditionally. Hofstatter and another investigative unit member, Mzilikazi wa Afrika, were, in Harber's words, 'let go'. Another member of the investigative unit and the 'rogue unit' stories' most ardent defender, Piet Rampedi, had already quit.

Daily Maverick journalist Marianne Thamm described the ombudsman's findings as 'damning' and concluded that the 'independence of the media has been abused' and the *Sunday Times* had been 'unethical and immoral'.

Today, besides some former *Sunday Times* investigative-unit journalists, the EFF and the Independent newspaper group, there appear to be very few people who have actually engaged with the 'rogue unit' narrative who still believe it existed.

❖

It wasn't just the *Sunday Times* that was drawn into the campaign. Over the years, a series of 'investigations' into the 'rogue unit' were done, some at the behest of Tom Moyane – appointed commissioner of SARS by Jacob Zuma, and the man who ousted Van Loggerenberg, Pillay and Richer.

Telita Snyckers, a former SARS executive and now an independent expert on illicit trade, wrote in the *Financial Mail* in December 2020, 'By all accounts, the unit was established lawfully. Legal opinions were obtained prior to its establishment, it was reflected on the SARS organogram, its cost centre was properly and transparently accounted for and annually audited, its members received IRP5 tax certificates, vacant positions were openly advertised and it was subject to the same checks and balances that applied to other SARS units.'

Richer points out that every state department had an intelligence capacity, and that the customs and tax laws gave SARS 'quite considerable powers … and all of this was built within that framework'.

In her report, Snyckers addresses the various investigations that were done into the unit. She notes that Advocate Muzi Sikhakhane compiled a report at SARS's behest 'without once interviewing a single member of the unit about the issue'. 'SARS recently (finally but quietly) distanced itself from the Sikhakhane report,' she notes.

Another report, by Judge Frank Kroon, a former chair of the SARS advisory board, found the unit to be unlawful but Kroon later confessed that he had relied on Sikhakhane's report. He issued an apology to unit members and their families.

A report by KPMG which reached the same conclusion was subsequently withdrawn by the international auditing firm itself, and several of its senior executives in South Africa quit.

The inspector-general of intelligence also compiled a damning report, which was set aside in 2020. And, finally, public protector Busisiwe Mkhwebane's finding that there was a 'rogue unit' was dismissed by the North Gauteng high court in late 2020. The court said 'she allowed her important office to be used to try and resuscitate a long-dead fake news propaganda fiction'.

Snyckers concluded, 'These were the reports which detractors of the [rogue] unit rely on – and now every single one of them has been discounted. Or, looked at from the other side, there is not a single authoritative report that suggests the existence of any scallywag units at SARS; not a single piece of evidence, simply circular references that all come from the same sources.'

In February 2020 the National Prosecuting Authority (NPA), no longer dancing to Jacob Zuma's tune, withdrew all charges that had been filed in courts in connection with the 'rogue unit' or Gordhan's time at SARS.

The various attacks on SARS, Gordhan and senior executives suggest a coordinated and comprehensive campaign. But why?

Richer points to a compliance programme developed by SARS that was designed to bring non-compliant taxpayers and industries into the tax net. 'Very prominent in that compliance programme ... was the tobacco industry, because [it] was non-compliant in terms of income tax, in terms of excise duties, in terms of smuggling issues, and so on. And so the idea was to start to really focus on the tobacco industry, and that seems to have been the beginning of our downfall, because the vested interests that seem to have been playing out in that industry were far more varied than we realised. And so we were taking on a lot more than we'd anticipated.'

Richer was involved in the creation of the compliance pro-gramme as head of strategy, the investigative audit fell under Pillay, and Van Loggerenberg was directly managing the investigations units involved in the process. 'That just began the targeting, and then I think other issues just played into it,' says Richer, saying they were 'a thorn in the side of the whole looting/state-capture initiative'.

'I think they began to realise the same thing that Pravin had years before: that if you can control the tax authority, you can guide the whole nature of the state. We thought initially that they wouldn't go after the ATM – they would just mug the people withdrawing the money. But eventually they decided to go for the ATM itself. So SARS obviously became a target. And then I guess … it was just a question of finding an excuse, something that you could build some sort of scandal around. And they focused on this issue of this unit.'

Van Loggerenberg compares the 'rogue unit' propaganda process to a series of paper cuts, which were administered to SARS by a unit of the State Security Agency (SSA, whose mandate is to provide the government with intelligence on domestic and foreign threats or potential threats to national stability, security and safety, and which subsequent events suggest had itself gone rogue), the tobacco industry and 'people in the "tender-preneur" space who knew we were onto them – the Zumas knew, the pals of Zuma knew, the Guptas knew. So the fact of the matter is we were pretty isolated and we had made a lot of enemies by early 2014. Then along comes Ivan and announces we're looking into Nkandla.

'If you look at this as paper cuts, paper cuts, paper cuts, and then the big sharks come in, and the first great white that comes in for a bite is Tom Moyane. And he takes a big bite … me, Pete [Richer], Ivan.

'And then that gets layered with the Sikhakhane report, KPMG, Kroon … and these things get layered and layered and layered. And then, ultimately, I think they won. They captured the institution, they broke it and changed it and repurposed it to what they wanted it to be.'

Pillay says a lot of people had been 'wounded' by SARS investigations, 'and naturally they began to connect with each other, and they connected to politicians'.

He believes a meeting he had with Zuma – whom he knew from their shared struggle backgrounds – to, in part, raise the suggestion that his office was interfering in the work of SARS 'might have speeded things up'. 'In retrospect, I think these things might have confirmed to Zuma that we were keeping an eye on him. In fact, most of the things we got from journalists and, as a concerned public servant, I went to him and said, "This is what we are hearing." I thought that in doing … that, I would be saying to him, "Listen, I'm aware, other people are aware. You should tread carefully." But it didn't happen.'

Pillay recalls getting a message from a journalist who'd been tipped off by a minister in Zuma's cabinet that 'you guys are going to be dealt with, and you're going to be dealt with thoroughly so that you will be forced out and nobody in South Africa will touch you'.

Van Loggerenberg says that if Moyane hadn't been appointed to replace Oupa Magashula in 2014, 'we would have weathered the storm, I can assure you, because it wasn't our first rodeo. But what Moyane did was he took us all out of the equation. The ability to bat the balls out of the park was taken away.'

Pillay says 'it was a difficult time because we knew that as much as we were attacked, and were directly under pressure, we knew that part of that attack was against Pravin'. 'And perhaps even a small part of it against [former finance minister] Trevor Manuel, and the legacy of Trevor and the treasury. And we were conscious that we didn't want to make things even more problematic for Pravin, so we would be very circumspect about direct contacts.

'And, obviously, Pravin would have done all he could behind the scenes to help – speak to lawyers, speak to other people who could provide us with resources. The first year was incredibly difficult … Zuma and his people made it so abundantly clear that they were up to no good.'

Gordhan is blunt in his assessment: it had everything to do with the 'tobacco mafia' and 'everything to do with the fact that Edward Zuma is part of that mafia. So a lot of that is protecting him and his malfeasance'. 'You have the rogue elements within the media as well – Mzilikazi and Piet Rampedi – who thought they were on a mission of their own … who still think they're on a mission of their own.'

The consequences for SARS were devastating. Richer says the 'rogue unit' scandal provided 'an excuse to strip out the investigative capability and the investigative direction'. 'A tax investigator and a tax auditor takes years to develop. It's a skill. If you think of trying to investigate tax evasion … the maths would baffle even a maths professor. It's just hugely complex. So it takes time to train people like that. And so the devastation that was done in smashing those units is going to take still quite a few years for SARS to recover from. And, of course, in that time, compliance levels are dropping. If you think, Pravin took ten years to get those compliance levels to the levels that he managed, it'll take another ten years to get them back up again.'

Van Loggerenberg says that after the *Sunday Times* unit's reporting 'every single crook in the country that was in litigation with SARS tried … the rogue unit defence'. 'Then it got a new life of its own … this thing's never going to go away. I can tell you, we've all been branded for life ... People like Rampedi and Malema talk about a rogue unit as if it still exists.'

He adds, 'You know SARS was never perfect, make no mistake, but, hell, it was going to go places, and it's very easy to break something like that because it's so fragile. And now to try and repair it, that's going to be like trying to stick a Ming vase together with superglue. It's always going to have cracks.'

The personal consequences for those dragged through the mud were equally devastating.

Pillay, who left SARS in 2015, says that 'when it's happening you don't think too much about how you're actually feeling, and you don't want to feel too much because it can immobilise you'. 'You're aware that not as many people phone as before. You're aware that some people ... take abrupt turns and walk away from you when they see you. And those who are brave enough to still see you, they must park far away and walk to the house or meet in some secluded spot. So, obviously, there's that awareness that you're an outlaw.

'It's painful for the families, very painful. Some of us have been used to something like this for decades. But our families didn't ask for this. And the toll on families across the board has been quite high.'

Pillay and the others suffered financially when SARS refused to pay any legal costs. 'There's got to be some sort of amends for all the people who were unfairly targeted ... and those amends must be made by the state and by the ANC. We're still battling with the legal costs. It's a lot of money – the estimate is about R9 million. And then some of us have been without formal employment for five, six years. Reputations have been tarnished. So there's a sense in which that should be made right.'

Richer was suspended from SARS in December 2014. After he challenged the suspension in court, it was overturned, but 'SARS simply reinstituted the suspension and it dragged on again'. In May 2015, he left the organisation after coming to a separation agreement.

He says 'the nature of the attack [was] designed to destroy reputations'. 'Somebody with my background and the positions I held in government would probably be getting an ambassadorship somewhere [now]. Nothing spectacular, maybe Kuwait. That's normally how one's career [would end but] not if you have that kind of stuff hanging over you.

'Under normal circumstances, Ivan Pillay would be a commissioner or an ambassador. [Now], there's no chance. His reputation is completely destroyed. Even if the evidence has vindicated him, these things just hang on.

'It's even worse for younger people who are much earlier in their careers ... and many of them don't have the struggle type of background that says, okay, let's just plug on. They're career auditors, career investigators. I think quite a few of them actually had nervous breakdowns, and they've had divorces and things. So the personal cost has been huge.'

13
The Cabal

In October 2018, EFF deputy president Floyd Shivambu decided to pick away at a long-standing South African sore: the relationship between African and Indian.

Tensions between the two groups have sometimes been a source of conflict and have occasionally erupted into violence, the most notable being the horrifying assaults on Indians in Durban in 1949 – the so-called Cato Manor riots. More than 140 people died in violence that lasted three days and was reportedly cheered by white residents. Certainly, the police response was tardy and half-hearted.

South Africans might generally have since embraced the constitution's edicts on non-racialism, but that hasn't stopped populist politicians from occasionally attempting to exploit historical grudges.

In a lengthy and rambling blog post – which he modestly described as an 'insightful polemic' – Shivambu resurrected suggestions that a 'cabal' had had undue influence over the Mass Democratic Movement (MDM) in the 1980s and early 1990s.

But his real target was Pravin Gordhan, and in that respect Shivambu was anything but nuanced: 'The Cabal was basically an

Indian Cabal that was put in place to slander the character and standing of African comrades in the MDM, and it was led by Pravin Gordhan,' said the EFF's number two. 'Even when the MDM was confronted with a common enemy – the white settler colonial state – Pravin was keen on sowing divisions within MDM structures, [to] undermine and denigrate the role of mostly African leadership in the mass movement. The essence of Pravin's ideological and political outlook was and remains collaboration with existing capitalist interests and undermining the overall leadership of the movement.'

He continued, 'One of the distinct features of the Cabal under the leadership of Pravin was domestication of African comrades. And this phenomenon continues to define how he relates to African leadership in the ANC up to this day.'

Shivambu argued that the 'cabal' still exists and named its 'inner circle' as Gordhan, Ismail Momoniat (whom he described as 'the Deputy Director General in National Treasury responsible for everything'), and reserve bank deputy governor Kuben Naidoo. Former finance minister Trevor Manuel 'provides the link between the Cabal and the Capitalist establishment'.

Shivambu brought his blog to a lurid climax, warning of the 'fragrant [sic] dominance of the Pravin led Cabal in South Africa'.

His article was based largely on a curious document in the O'Malley Archives called the Report of the Commission on the Cabal. The archives contain documents and transcripts of the more than two thousand hours of interviews Padraig O'Malley conducted with South Africans about the transition to democracy. O'Malley has also written a biography on Mac Maharaj.

The Report of the Commission on the Cabal document begins with a conclusion: 'The problems of disunity within the ranks of the MDM due to the manipulating role of certain Indians and Whites regarded as leaders in the struggle, has reached a level of such seriousness that it is clear that we need to address it immediately and decisively.'

It explains that 'a commission was mandated to discuss the problem and make recommendations towards its resolution' and adds, 'We would however like to stress that this document is neither meant for public consumption nor is it intended to serve as a communiqué to be distributed.'

It's unclear who authored this supposed report, dated 14 March 1990, and the copy in the O'Malley Archives ends in the middle of a sentence. The site warns that the document is 'incomplete'.

This apparently didn't put Shivambu off his stride and he suggested that 'it appears that Mr [Mac] Maharaj drafted the report'. Maharaj, speaking to the *Mail & Guardian*'s Franny Rabkin in March 2019, said he had 'no knowledge of, or participation in, the preparation of this so-called report'. The newspaper quoted him as saying that it was a 'very strange document to [appear] in March 1990 – just after the ANC, MK and SACP were unbanned'.

'Over the years as a Congress activist, PG had contributed to building organisations and capacity both in the underground and in the Mass Democratic Movement, working with comrades from all communities in many anti-apartheid campaigns. Insofar as this purported report maligns any of the people named in it, it is a complete distortion of the reality. It is a misuse of the document to dub Pravin as a mischief-maker and a cabalist,' he told the newspaper.

In the transcript of an interview in the same archives, Billy Nair tells O'Malley that the allegations of a cabal were a 'cheap trick to divide the organisation and to make up for the lack of political maturity'. 'Some people not conversant with the dynamics of the movement felt that there was a secret organisation, a cabal operating within the Indian Congress or the UDF because it took a particular position on issues,' Nair told O'Malley. 'Pravin Gordhan was accused of being a leader of the cabal. We said, "OK, what did he say, what did he do?" If you talk about a leader of the cabal, let's look at the substance and tease that out.'

Not one to pull punches, Nair described the accusation as stemming from 'petty jealousy'. He added, 'These were immature elements within the organisation who nitpicked because they lacked the capacity for leadership.'

Kumi Naidoo, a Durban-born human-rights and environmental activist who gained international renown as the executive director of Greenpeace, wrote his doctoral thesis at the University of Oxford on Indian political resistance in Durban between 1979 and 1996. In it he teases out the origins of the cabal allegations.

He points to conflicts in NIC and UDF politics over issues such as boycotts and the relationship with the tricameral parliament, and says that these tensions manifested themselves in different ways at the local level. 'For example, some Chatsworth activists adopted an antagonistic position towards the potential of "control by the town grouping" led by Pravin Gordhan.'

He cites criticism that the NIC was too 'issue-orientated', and 'cliqueism' and 'infighting' as among the perceived concerns. 'In particular, an observation was made that the organisation's practice was dominated by a "Chemist Grouping" [Gordhan was a chemist], and a few people who met regularly at his pharmacy were believed to unduly influence the organisation.'

It was this chemist/town grouping that became known as the cabal. 'A joke at one factory suggested that NIC policy under Dr Monty Naicker was "just what the doctor ordered", but under George Sewpersad, a lawyer, NIC policy was "just what the chemist [in reference to Gordhan] ordered!"'

Naidoo says that some senior NIC executives 'claimed that they were excluded from activities, seldom notified of meetings, and were not consulted on key issues'.

He points out that five Chatsworth branches and the one Phoenix branch were part of the ANC's first regional conference in 1991, 'when four Indians were elected to serve on the regional executive committee'. 'Significantly, two NIC/ANC stalwarts, Billy Nair and Pravin Gordhan, were defeated, presumably because of their cabal associations.'

Sandy Africa says that in the late 1980s 'there was a feeling that too much power and influence aggregated around [Gordhan's] person and [that's where the claims] crept in of him being the leader of a so-called cabal within the NIC. And people also argue that this extended beyond the NIC to other parts of the UDF and the then Mass Democratic Movement.'

She says it was suggested that Gordhan was able to 'influence decisions and bypass the structures and a lot of disquiet started to develop around that. But this was an unfortunately divided time in politics. And so ... his name was sometimes associated with undue influence, perhaps even divisiveness, although I didn't experience him as being a divisive leader in any way.'

Mpho Scott believes the accusation arose from circumstances at the time. The climate was such that every decision couldn't be debated with everyone who might have an interest in it. 'Some expected a super-democratic environment to take place where you'll have a thousand people, everyone in one room, to discuss certain things. But if you do that, then you're going to prison ... you'll get killed.'

He believes the focus on Gordhan was because he was 'key in terms of some of those structures that were seen working with the cabal ... When people mentioned the cabal, even if they mentioned twelve or thirteen people, his name was there'.

In June 2018 Shivambu had objected to Ismail Momoniat's

'repeated presence' in parliamentary finance committee meetings and described the treasury deputy-director as a 'non-African' who undermined Africans. His comments were roundly dismissed by many struggle veterans, who pointed to Momoniat's long and courageous history of activism.

The man himself appears remarkably sanguine about it but prefers not to engage in the debate. He does, however, also believe the cabal accusations arose from the extraordinary circumstances of the time. 'The point is that we would, of course, have had secret meetings and so on in the days of apartheid. We didn't announce to the security police that we were organising ... and so, yes, there was some tension. When there were differences, people said, "You guys are a cabal and you guys are imposing your views on us." I was also accused of being part of the cabal.

'I think we had to operate in a particular way. And we operated on the basis of need to know. We didn't announce to everyone that we had contact with the ANC [or that we had] got our secret cells. I mean, you would've been charged with treason. But before you even got charged, you would've been beaten to a pulp.'

He believes part of the problem may have been Gordhan's style at the time, which he describes as 'very strong'. 'I think his style would piss off people and make people resentful.'

Abba Omar says 'there's no doubt that the Indian activists were better resourced'. 'We all came from, at best, sort of lower-middle-class households. We were able to raise a little bit more money, more resources, and there was often this accusation that Indian activists were dominating the resources. There was a community research unit [CRU] that was in existence. There was the accusation that Indians were dominating the resources of CRU.

'I think Joe Slovo captured the cabal issue well at a meeting in Lusaka with the MDM. As he was leaving the meeting with

[Desmond] Tutu, he said to him, "You know, this cabal thing is a bit like [whether] you believe in God or not."'

Slovo explained that some people believed there was control by a cabal, while others said it was just an organisational way of doing things. 'And it's like God, you know: things happen, maybe you think God did it,' said Slovo.

'So I think it's been overstated,' Omar concludes. 'Sometimes there may have been a slight insensitivity among some of the Indian comrades. So maybe they've been slightly patronising at times, but I think people were genuinely committed to non-racialism and wanted to work with African comrades as much as possible.'

Gordhan is also of the view that the charge arose from the particular conditions of the time: 'You know, small groups of people did operate [and] some did get pissed off because they weren't part of it or they felt the influence of all of these developments. And when it was convenient, it later became a swear word.

'But as you know, every political or social formation of any kind will have what today you call factions, or groups of people who share a particular interest. So somebody wants to vote for Jonathan as a chair of the soccer club. Others want to vote for Chris. You'll have a support base and he'll have a support base. Each of you will meet secretly to see how you can mobilise others. So, essentially, you have two cabals operating.'

✦

But why was the cabal narrative resurrected in 2018?

Nomboniso Gasa, adjunct professor of public law and senior research associate at the Centre for Law and Society at the University of Cape Town, wrote on the issue for *City Press* in November 2018 – the month after Shivambu's blog. Her article was headlined

'"Indian cabal" narrative is to protect the looting project'.

She pointed out that by virtue of his previous positions as SARS commissioner and finance minister, Gordhan has been on the frontline of the fight against those who pillaged the state. Addressing the ANC, she added, 'There is a need to give personal and political support to whomever range themselves against the thieves. That would be leadership. Instead, Gordhan is subjected to a range of attacks, some of them completely racist, personalised or inaccurate. Some of these attacks have relied heavily on South Africa's race politics, distorting the history of the ANC, the Mass Democratic Movement (MDM) and the United Democratic Front (UDF), especially in the 1980s, and the so-called cabal.'

She concluded that 'this is a political project ... to undermine any attempts to halt corruption'.

Shivambu is not alone in pursuing this project. In recent years there have been repeated attempts to blow life into it from a range of individuals.

14

Smoke Without Fire

Journalists in South Africa are fond of the old saying that there's no smoke without fire, meaning that if you're routinely hearing rumours or allegations about somebody, there's probably some truth to them. A news editor confronted with this would shoot back with another smoke-related newsroom cliché: 'Okay, but where's the smoking gun?' He or she might have added, 'Don't come back until you find it.'

But two stains on the country's media in the post-democratic age suggest that the latter aspect of that exchange – which demands plausible confirmation before a story gets anywhere near being printed – had been abandoned, at least in some circles and circumstances. In other words, stories were finding their way into print in some products without anything like the fact-checking process that has been traditionally required of journalists.

Both of those stains played a role in the efforts by the state-capture looters and others to fight back against Pravin Gordhan.

The first was the *Sunday Times*'s investigative unit – and particularly its coverage of the SARS 'rogue unit', which we've already described. The second is the controversial stewardship of the Independent newspaper group of Iqbal Survé, a self-styled entrepreneur and 'ardent philanthropist' (according to his company's website), who appears to have exaggerated a great deal of his background, including his major claim to fame: that he was a personal friend of and physician to Nelson Mandela. Asked by journalist Terry Bell about apparent discrepancies in his claims, Survé maintained that he owed nobody an explanation about his relationship with Mandela. 'Our relationship, both personal and professional, is not one I wish to flaunt publicly,' said Survé.

And there's a thread that runs through both media stains: Piet Rampedi and Mzilikazi wa Afrika, former members of the *Sunday Times* investigative unit who subsequently found a home at Independent.

Stephan Hofstatter's partial mea culpa at Love Books stands in sharp contrast to the attitude of Rampedi, who's been vocal in defence of the investigative unit's stories. Rampedi quit the *Sunday Times* in March 2016. His resignation letter, published on the website Uncensored ('Stories that Media Ignore'), reads in part: 'The reasons for my resignation are, among other things, what I consider to be unethical conduct by the Sunday Times editors and/or Times Media Group in entering into an underhanded deal with Ivan Pillay, Johann Loggerenberg [sic], representatives of Minister Pravin Gordhan and other former SARS officials that my colleagues and I have been investigating for past two years for their alleged roles in the setting up and running of the rogue unit.'

Anton Harber, in his book *So, For The Record*, which interrogates the activities of the investigative unit, says that the resignation came after Rampedi heard that *Sunday Times* editor Bongani Siqoko had agreed to meet Johann van Loggerenberg to hear his side of the story.

(Rampedi didn't respond to requests for an interview for this book, nor did Survé.)

Rampedi and Wa Afrika – who was 'let go' by the *Sunday Times* some two years after Rampedi had resigned, as it became evident how poor the 'rogue unit' reporting had been – were, unsurprisingly, snapped up by Survé's Independent group, which has in recent years targeted Gordhan, in part by attempting to resurrect the rogue-unit narrative. The pen of Rampedi has been wielded routinely to this end.

Newspapers in the Independent group include big-city dailies such as the *Cape Argus*, the *Cape Times* and the *Daily Voice* in Cape Town, *The Mercury* in Durban, *The Star* in Johannesburg and the *Pretoria News*; and weekenders such as the *Sunday Independent* and the *Sunday Tribune*.

Rampedi's loyalty to Survé and his pursuit of his boss's causes were subsequently rewarded with a promotion to editor of the *Pretoria News* – although, with a reported circulation of just 1 800, it was perhaps not the greatest of rewards.

❖

On 9 October 2019, Survé's offices were raided by the Financial Sector Conduct Authority (FSCA), an arm of the treasury dedicated to enhancing the efficiency and integrity of financial markets, promoting fair customer treatment, and assisting in maintaining financial stability, among other things. It later explained that it had done so as part of an investigation into alleged 'prohibited trading practices (market manipulation)' in connection with one of Survé's companies.

Survé turned to the Independent's *Business Report*, which had effectively become his personal PR outlet, and it posted a video of him reacting during the raid, which he described as a 'political case'. He added that 'it's Pravin Gordhan behind this', and that the raid was designed to stop his newspapers from publishing reports about Gordhan, who by this stage was the minister of public enterprises.

Survé claimed that Judge Patrick Gamble, who'd granted the FSCA the order to carry out the raid, was associated with Gordhan and the DA. 'You went to a judge who's a friend of the DA and Pravin Gordhan. This is purely a fishing expedition on your part,' he said to an FSCA official in the office.

Judge Gamble has denied any association with Gordhan or the DA. A statement issued two days after the raid by the office of chief justice Mogoeng Mogoeng said: 'Neither the minister nor his department were … parties to the proceedings. [Gamble] has no affiliation nor membership with any political party, nor has he in the past.'

Gordhan dismissed the allegations as malicious and nonsensical. He doesn't know Judge Gamble. 'I didn't even know the name prior to [Survé's] mentioning it.'

That wasn't the only time that Survé had a go at Gordhan, or that his newspapers gave him a platform to do so.

Four days after the FSCA raid, reporters Sizwe Dlamini and Ayanda Mdluli claimed in the *Sunday Independent* that Gordhan was trying to influence the Mpati commission of inquiry into allegations of impropriety at the Public Investment Corporation (PIC), the state-owned R2-trillion-plus investor of public servants' pension funds, and Africa's largest asset manager. Among other things, the commission was looking into R4,3 billion in pension-fund money that the PIC controversially invested in Survé's company AYO Technology Solutions.

Dlamini and Mdluli (another who has subsequently been rewarded for his efforts with an editorship) quoted Survé describing Gordhan as a 'bully under the guise of fighting state capture'.

The media boss also claimed that 'on various separate occasions, Mr Gordhan had mentioned to people that if Independent Media stops reporting on the rogue unit and on the public protector he would intervene to stop the attacks on my group and myself'.

The reporters then claimed that 'a whistleblower, whose name is known to Independent Media, said in a letter to Sekunjalo Group [Survé's holding company] that Gordhan had met Mpati commissioners Gill Marcus and Emmanuel Lediga, and Eskom chairperson Jabu Mabuza at a restaurant in Pretoria where a decision was taken "to destroy you and your businesses".'

The letter allegedly read, 'The plan to [destroy] your credibility was discussed a few days before you testified at the commission. A meeting was held at the Fuma [sic] restaurant – Pretoria. In attendance were Gill Marcus, Pravin Gordhan (an aide of his left after a short while), assistant commissioner Emmanuel Lediga and Jabu Mabuza. At the meeting they discussed about the line and type of questions to be asked. A document was handed to Gill Marcus.'

Marcus had earned Survé's ire six months earlier, when he was giving evidence to the Mpati commission and she upbraided him for using the opportunity as 'a political platform'.

As had become the pattern in the newspapers' reporting on Survé, any response by people it was accusing was tagged on to the bottom of the report. In this case, Gordhan's lawyer, Tebogo Malatji, dismissed the allegations out of hand: 'Our client categorically denies the allegations contained in your query regarding a meeting allegedly held at Fuma [sic] restaurant in Pretoria. No such meeting took place. Our client rejects the allegations contained in your enquiry as malicious, derisive and false. Our client emphatically denies that he was part of any conspiracy or plans "to destroy Dr Iqbal Survé and his businesses", as you allege.'

The *Sunday Independent*'s story is an example of a technique used by unscrupulous journalists, in which a subject is given an opportunity to respond to an accusation, is drawn into a denial, and the smear is aired anyway. It goes as follows:

Journalist: 'Do you beat your wife?'

Subject X: 'No.'

Headline the next day: 'X denies he beats his wife'.

It wasn't the last time that Independent's journalists would use this technique. In time, Gordhan's media people took to sending out pre-emptive media releases, warning that they had received questions from Independent which had no basis in fact. In March 2020, for example, the department of public enterprises issued a statement under the heading 'Public Enterprises warns of fake news from Sunday Independent'.

It read, 'The Ministry of Public Enterprises must caution the media about news coverage that can be expected in the Sunday Independent newspaper tomorrow, which appears to be part of an ongoing campaign by the newspaper and a group of its so-called "investigative journalists" to again tarnish the reputations and work of good, honest public servants with baseless insinuation.'

It listed a series of questions sent to Nthabiseng Borotho, the ministry's chief of staff, by reporter Mzilikazi wa Afrika in which he asked her to confirm or deny a number of charges. They included allegations that she'd failed matric, that she'd previously worked for the SSA, and that she drove a 'state car – a Lexus – with a state-issued petrol card'. The journalist was evidently on what is known in the industry as a 'fishing expedition', firing off a series of questions in the hope of an answer that might be embarrassing for the subject.

The department pointed out that the time given to respond to the questions was 'unreasonable, unfair and wholly inadequate'. It added that 'Ms Borotho and the Ministry emphatically reject and deny these allegations and any insinuation in the newspaper's reporting that may arise from them', and pointed out that she had matriculated in 1997, had never worked for the SSA, and drove her own vehicle.

It added, 'These questions follow a well established method used by Mr Wa Afrika and others at the *Sunday Independent*, such as Mr Piet Rampedi, to malign and destroy the careers of honest, dedicated public officials and to undermine public institutions. The owner of the newspaper, Dr Iqbal Survé, also appears to be engaged in a public campaign against the Ministry and the Department.'

The newspaper and Independent's online editors appear to have responded to this tactic by turning to their opinion sections, where writers have greater licence to express their personal perspectives. The attacks have been vitriolic.

On 7 January 2021 the company's online site, IOL, did ratings of cabinet ministers. They were attributed to a 'staff reporter' and gave Gordhan one point out of a possible five. 'If Tito Mboweni is a liar, Pravin Gordhan is Pinocchio himself,' the rating began, and it concluded, 'At best Minister Gordhan has polarised the country and nation on his detestation for transformation and his intolerance of experienced, competent and qualified South Africans from all creeds and races.'

IOL added that the ratings had been compiled by the *Daily News*, a newspaper based in Durban, and Independent Media's investigations unit. The group investigations editor at the time was none other than Piet Rampedi.

The Star, in an editorial comment in March 2021, said of Gordhan that 'if he is not connecting the gossip dots or firing those who dare to question him, he is ducking and diving like a confused child who simply does not want to own up to his mistakes'. It also blithely repeated what the North Gauteng high court had described as 'long-dead fake news propaganda fiction', saying that his 'persistent defiance and refusal to take responsibility for his illegal activities at the [South African] Revenue Service, after illegally setting up a rogue unit that was used as an instrument to get back at his political opponents, is an exhibition of disrespect to our country'.

173

Professor Sipho Seepe, writing in *The Star* in December 2020, said of Gordhan's appearance before the Zondo commission, 'A man who has been riding the high horse of political morality was exposed to be nothing short of petty, jealous, racist and dangerous. For too long he has been allowed to level accusations against all.'

Revelations at the Zondo commission that the SSA paid Survé's African News Agency (ANA) R20 million have given rise to widespread speculation about what that money was intended to secure, and some finger-pointing at Independent journalists. In an astonishingly naive statement, ANA chief executive Vasantha Angamuthu admitted that 'in 2016/2017, ANA had a contract with the SSA to provide multimedia training for SSA analysts and interns across Africa, and to use its platforms, in particular the African Independent newspaper, to carry positive stories about South Africa and the South African government'.

Any such deal would once have been anathema to the newspaper group in question, but Angamuthu insisted there was nothing untoward about it and that she didn't believe the SSA had sinister intent.

The commission also heard that individual journalists had been paid by the SSA, but Van Loggerenberg is of the view that the original *Sunday Times* rogue-unit reporting and subsequent coverage by Rampedi wasn't funded. 'If you wanted a story in the *Sunday Times* in 2014, there was only one way to do it, and that was to access that so-called investigations team. And it was the easiest thing in the world, the easiest. I mean, why would you want to pay? And ... I honestly doubt that you needed to pay Piet one cent to write anything negative about Pravin Gordhan, Ivan Pillay, the South African Revenue Service, me or anybody else at that point in time. You didn't need to. All you needed to do was give him something that would withstand the low onus of printing a story, and he would run with it.

'Piet's gone so far now that if you can put together a document that expresses views on the shape of Pravin Gordhan's toenails, I'm sure you'd get it on the front page of the *Pretoria News*.'

Gordhan himself, asked about the fact that Survé's newspapers routinely attack him, is sanguine. 'It's very clear they belong to the stable of state capture, and [have set out to] to defend the corrupt and to attack those of us who are working in this administration.'

He's got to the point where he sometimes has to just ignore the 'wild allegations'. 'If I were to go and pursue every one of those, I'd be spending more time in court than anything else, [and] also using up state resources. I think Survé and company have painted themselves in their colours, and they must bear the consequences of that as we go on.'

❖

By 'and company', Gordhan might be referring to Survé's recent ideological bedfellows – the so-called RET forces, the EFF and public protector Busisiwe Mkhwebane – all of whom have also launched extraordinary and apparently baseless attacks on Gordhan.

The EFF, after initially supporting Gordhan when Jacob Zuma was trying to eject him from the cabinet, has turned on him viciously. Members of the EFF have taken to referring to Gordhan by his middle name, 'Jamnadas'. This appears to be a deliberate racial insult. Gordhan describes it as 'pure racism. And a mocking of people like myself'.

Ashwin Desai, professor of sociology at the University of Johannesburg, wrote in the *Daily Maverick* that the word isn't just a slang phrase: 'among the gangsters and prison numbers [inmates], it is a deliberate racial insult, one rung lower than the "c" word' – a reference to the reviled 'coolie' slur.

Malema has defended the practice: 'Whether the enemy likes it or not, the enemy cannot blame us. They must blame the mother and father of Jamnadas for naming him … down with Jamnadas, down!'

Some of the EFF's attempts to smear Gordhan have bordered on the comical. In October 2018, EFF 'commander-in-chief' Julius Malema opened a criminal case against Gordhan at the Brooklyn police station in Pretoria. According to a TimesLive report, the complaint contained allegations of money laundering, corruption, racketeering, fraud, contravention of the Intelligence Act and the Prevention and Combating of Corrupt Activities Act, and perjury. It also claimed that Gordhan's daughter, Anisha, was a beneficiary of state contracts.

Gordhan's spokesperson, Adrian Lackay, responded, 'Their so-called "charge sheet" is baseless, containing a set of lies, fake news and fabrications.'

The following day, News24 added weight to Lackay's comments when it fact-checked the EFF's charges. The party had made a series of sloppy and sometimes laughable errors. It had claimed that Gordhan operated an 'unlawful bank account' at the Royal Bank of Canada's Sherbrook branch in Montreal in the name of R Jamandas Gordhan. The News24 team found that the account number provided by the EFF didn't exist at the bank in question; that non-Canadian citizens could only apply for a bank account in the country if they were in the process of immigrating, had a residence permit or held a student or work visa (and Gordhan's office said he had no plans to emigrate and pointed out that he held South African citizenship only); that the EFF got Gordhan's first initial and the spelling of his middle name wrong (his full names are Pravin Jamnadas Gordhan), and that the branch is not in Sherbrook, Montreal, but in the town of Sherbrooke in southern Quebec, 156km away.

In addition, the News24 team established that the allegations against Gordhan's daughter Anisha were without substance. These included the claim that 'her company', Vox Telecommunications, had done extensive business with the government as a result of Gordhan's tenure as finance minister. Anisha Gordhan was in fact employed as an investment banker at Investec Bank at the time. Investec is a shareholder in Vox, which 'necessitated Anisha Gordhan's position as a non-executive director at Vox', reported News24. In other words, Vox wasn't her company, and she wouldn't have benefited from any government contracts it might have secured.

The party's obsession with Gordhan turned ugly in June 2019, when several of its red-overall-clad MPs stormed and crowded around the parliamentary podium where Gordhan, then the minister of public enterprises, was making his budget speech. In December 2020, a parliamentary disciplinary committee found sixteen EFF MPs guilty of misconduct for the incident. The committee recommended that two of them be suspended without pay and the remaining fourteen be fined various amounts.

Former minister Derek Hanekom, who alongside Gordhan took on state capture under Zuma, says 'the reason I think that he's been so viciously attacked is precisely because he's such a big threat to people who are facing prison sentences or who want to continue with their looting'. 'It will not deter him, and he will not relent, but, having experienced quite a bit of it myself, it's not a nice experience to be on the receiving end of racial attacks and to be accused of being the agent of white monopoly capital and more than that …'

He points out that the EFF treated Gordhan as a 'hero at one point. And then the next point – as soon as he seemed to be getting closer to what they've been doing – suddenly he becomes a villain. He becomes a subject of racial attacks from the EFF side.'

Hanekom adds that there have been elements in the ANC – such as the so-called RET grouping – who also indulged in these attacks.

'But the EFF did it quite blatantly. It was a very quick transition from them having called for Zuma to go and "pay back the money" [for the public funds spent on his private Nkandla estate]. And then it becomes increasingly clear that they may also have stolen … and Pravin is the one who is most likely to stand in their way and have them exposed. So it changes, and it changes quite quickly.'

A long-standing colleague of Gordhan's who's in government says the EFF has aligned 'with a particular faction in the ANC and I have no doubt they will merge with [suspended ANC secretary-general] Ace [Magashule] and others, and will have an alliance to even protect the public protector when it comes to a vote [on her being removed from office]'.

'The EFF are masters at propaganda. I think that the EFF is also quite racist. [It] understands that in a propaganda war, you need sym-bols – you need to say [Johann] "Rupert" for whites; you need to say "Pravin" and play the Indian card and reinforce it. Pravin is seen as someone who's fighting corruption, and they've aligned themselves with a faction that doesn't want Pravin to succeed. These guys are very consistent. They'll keep on repeating it, and also then calling him "Jamnadas". I mean, they are really flagrantly racist.'

He believes a second factor is that 'they're trying to show that Cyril is not his own man'. This, he believes, is another reason why Rupert and Gordhan are consistently portrayed by the party as controlling Ramaphosa.

And, finally, 'I think the other reason why they've targeted Pravin is they have their own conduct to defend.'

There have been countless other attacks on Gordhan by the EFF, but to date none of its allegations appear to have any substance. Malema didn't respond to a request by the authors for an interview.

Perhaps one of the most extraordinary allegations against Gordhan came from within the ANC itself, when former state security minister – and Zuma ally – Bongani Bongo claimed that he'd fallen ill after a meeting with Gordhan and had had to seek treatment in Cuba. 'I was given poison,' he said in a television interview in November 2019.

Gordhan's then spokesperson, Sam Mkokeli, responded to the allegation by saying it was 'ridiculously foolish' and the former minister 'must be hallucinating'. And Bongo was forced to cut his Cuba trip short when he was ordered to hand himself over to the Hawks on corruption charges. Bongo was subsequently tried and controversially acquitted by the equally controversial Western Cape Judge President John Hlophe.

◈

Several other serious allegations levelled at Gordhan have also been dismissed. These include fraud charges laid by former NPA boss Shaun Abrahams and, as mentioned, public protector Busisiwe Mkhwebane's various findings against Gordhan. But why? Why have these people lined up against Gordhan?

His former deputy in the finance ministry, Mcebisi Jonas, points out that the treasury – headed up by the finance minister – is the 'repository of data and knowledge about what's happening in the public system'. That, he says, ranges from data on forensic audits to maladministration and misappropriation of resources. 'And if you add, on top of that, the role that PG played as the commissioner of SARS, which again is another area where you get lots of information, sometimes uncomfortable information ...'

A second element would be Gordhan's personality. 'PG is one of those who will tell it like it is ... he won't sugar-coat and that kind of stuff.' This doesn't go down well with people who would prefer that you 'soft-pedal on their weaknesses'.

Jonas also points out that the new administration has set out to combat corruption and state capture, to map a new trajectory for the economy, to reform state institutions, and then to align social policy with those objectives. Who in government, he asks, would be best placed to drive it towards those objectives? Not many, 'and among those few people, PG is probably topmost'. He believes, therefore, that the attacks on Gordhan might be a 'proxy for another war' being waged against President Cyril Ramaphosa.

Mandla Nkomfe, a former Gauteng member of the executive committee for finance who's been hired as an adviser by Gordhan since 2014, agrees that 'part of it is that he's just a straight guy' but also that he calls out people about their conduct. 'And people don't like it because I think he embarrasses them by the way he does things ... and he is not the type of person that you can say, "Let's go out for coffee." He's straightforward: "I don't do coffee. If you want to see me, come to the office."'

Pete Richer agrees that Gordhan can 'rub people up the wrong way very easily. He's got a sharp tongue. He's got a very emphatic manner and he can piss people off very easily.'

Nkomfe adds, 'But there's a silent majority [of] ordinary, salt-of-the-earth activists who are really behind him and who send him messages of support. But I must say it's not been easy, particularly that period of 2016 and 2017. That was rough. It's still rough today.'

Richer points out that 'when Pravin was minister of finance, he was very tight on controlling expenditure and was very critical of fellow ministers who seemed to be wasting'. He's always been 'very strong' about corruption.

Judge Thumba Pillay believes Gordhan is 'caught up as an unwilling victim in the factional battles now consuming the ruling party', which is 'a great pity and sadly to the country's detriment'.

Derek Hanekom describes the attacks on Gordhan as 'brutal'. 'It hasn't been easy for him or his family. It's partly because of the kind of support he gets from some of us that he's able to say, "Look, there's a bigger task out there," but when you've given most of your life to liberating our country and making our country a better place for all, and these attacks come from the very people whom you stood for, it hurts; it obviously hurts.'

Ivan Pillay, reflecting on the nature of the attacks, says, 'One of the things about South Africans [is that] the facts don't matter. What matters is, "Can I use what you're telling me? Does it serve my interest?"'

In other words, in South Africa there apparently *is* smoke without fire.

15

Mr Charming

Jacob Zuma and Pravin Gordhan have been positioned as polar opposites in the state-capture project. For many, Zuma has become a symbol of corruption and cronyism, a conniving crook who sold South Africa on a platter to a band of greedy brothers, while Gordhan is seen as honourable and heroic: principled, moral and courageous, Mr Clean.

Sandy Africa, a comrade of Gordhan's in the struggle and now an associate professor in the department of political sciences at the University of Pretoria, says, 'I suppose it has been partly because he sat in those institutions which started ... to uncover certain things ... and wasn't afraid to use his leverage and his positions to question and to bring people to account. And, of course, the media likes to amplify. And so he became amplified as the antithesis of what Jacob Zuma stood for. And it's just kind of a nice, dramatic polarity, I suppose, to present to the public.'

As Africa suggests, the binary is journalistic convenience. But when you get into the nitty-gritty details of what happened during the nine years of Zuma's presidency, it's difficult to see it any other way.

The shadow of corruption has hung over Zuma since 2003, when the then NPA head, Bulelani Ngcuka, said there was a prima facie case of corruption against him. Zuma insisted on his day in court to prove his innocence – but almost two decades later, he's done everything in his power to stay out of court where he'd face hundreds of fraud and corruption charges. He's also lurched, in the meantime, from scandal to scandal.

His cheerleaders are Ace Magashule, who stands accused of corruption, money-laundering and fraud related to the asbestos project during his time as premier of the Free State; the disgraced Carl Niehaus, a former ANC spokesperson turned national joke; and, more recently, the EFF's Julius Malema, who once threatened to kill for Zuma, then became his fiercest critic, and now drinks tea and takes selfies with the former president.

During his tenure as president, Zuma used his extensive powers to fill his cabinet with loyalists, and deployed minions to head up institutions like the NPA and SARS, which effectively weakened any law-enforcement apparatus that might clamp down on corruption. For nine years he was, as veteran journalist Max du Preez famously described him, a one-man wrecking ball.

Gordhan stood firm when the wrecking ball targeted him and the treasury – although he wasn't the only one. Civil-society activists, investigative journalists, independent media like the *Daily Maverick*, whistleblowers, incorruptible public servants and honourable cabinet ministers, notably Nhlanhla Nene, stood shoulder to shoulder with Gordhan to expose the rot and push back against corruption. But it's Gordhan who has come to be seen as Zuma's foil, the poster child of the anti-corruption forces.

Zuma's firing of Gordhan as finance minister in 2014, and moving him to the local-government portfolio, was an attempt to neutralise him politically. And it worked for a while as Gordhan got to grips with his new portfolio. But then Zuma, who brought his chess skills into politics and prided himself on always being a few moves ahead of his opponents, exposed his queen. In his biggest political blunder, he fired Nene in 2015, and in so doing, he unleashed a political and economic tsunami.

We'll never know precisely when Zuma lost his way and went astray, but we have a very good idea when Gordhan realised that it was time to come out swinging. Nene's axing breathed fire into Gordhan. It also galvanised the anti-Zuma camp – within and outside of the ANC – into action.

Zuma was forced to reappoint Gordhan as minister of finance but it was evident that from that moment the two men had become fierce political foes.

◈

What is often forgotten is that Gordhan and Zuma haven't always been each other's nemesis. They were once comrades, whose lives had been intersecting since the 1970s when the enemy wasn't each other but the apartheid state. 'Yes,' says Gordhan, 'I know Zuma from 1974 … Today, of course, he would persecute me, but we go back a long, long way.'

The two men, who coincidentally share a birthday – 12 April – both hail from KwaZulu-Natal. Jacob Gedleyihlekisa Zuma was born in 1942 in Nkandla, and Pravin Jamnadas Gordhan came into the world seven years later in Durban, about 250 kilometres from Zuma's homestead in the north of the province.

They had different paths into activism. Zuma had no formal schooling and was recruited into MK by Moses Mabhida in 1959 and participated in sabotage operations. He was arrested in 1963, when he was only 21 years old, near Zeerust in today's North West province and sentenced to ten years' imprisonment for conspiring to overthrow the government. He didn't receive a single visitor during his entire ten-year stretch on Robben Island. When he came off the island in 1973, he set up underground networks to recruit for MK and arranged for the new soldiers to go to Mozambique for military training.

Gordhan, on the other hand, had become politically conscious at university and worked his way into the NIC, the ANC and the SACP underground. His focus was on mass mobilisation and building community organisations. Gordhan and his circle of comrades would meet political prisoners who were released from Robben Island and sent to Durban, and they built up a relationship with former prisoners like Mandla Judson Kuzwayo, Sunny Singh, Mac Maharaj and, of course, Jacob Zuma. Yousuf Vawda says, 'Zuma worked closely with us and we considered ourselves to be part of those [ANC] structures, so technically under that discipline.'

Gordhan and his comrades Yunus Mahomed, Roy Padayachie and Vawda ferried Zuma from Durban to Pietermaritzburg at various stages to meet Harry Gwala, 'the Lion of the Midlands', who was Zuma's MK commander. Vawda recalls one of those trips. 'I didn't have my own transportation, so I had to lie to my brother, who had a car, to say we needed it to go to some lecture in Pietermaritzburg. We picked up Zuma outside the Durban Transport Department – he was working there as a handyman or something – and then drove him to meet with Harry Gwala. We came back a couple of hours later and brought him back home.'

When Gwala was arrested in 1975, Zuma decided it was time to leave the country. According to Aboobaker, a member of Gordhan's group helped spirit Zuma out of Durban and into Swaziland.

Gordhan was working as a pharmacist at a branch of the King Edward VIII Hospital when Zuma popped his head through the hatch where medicines were dispensed. Gordhan recalls, 'He said, "I need to see you," and then he said, "I need some money." We took a walk to Standard Bank in Grey Street and I [withdrew] a few hundred rands, and that was the cash I think with which he left the country at that time." Gordhan adds, with studied understatement, 'It's a very different Zuma that we meet subsequently.'

Zuma and Thabo Mbeki were arrested in Swaziland the following year but a high-level ANC delegation managed to negotiate their release and Zuma was sent to Mozambique, where he held various positions in the movement, including commanding the Mandla Judson Kuzwayo unit, which was made up of Yunus and Moe Shaik and Jayendra Naidoo, and which cooperated with Gordhan's Providence unit from time to time.

Ivan Pillay, who went into exile in Swaziland in 1977, recalls, 'By the time I came out of the country, Zuma was already a member of the [ANC] national executive, but based in Mozambique. In about 1979 I was moved to the political section and Zuma also became part of that. He was our senior.'

Pillay had four or five formal meetings with Zuma each year, although he was never personally close to him – 'I never had a meal with Zuma.' 'We'd go into Mozambique illegally, have a meeting and then come back. I always saw him as an ambitious person who was prepared to use his ethnicity to his advantage, and it was a big advantage,' says Pillay. 'There was a relatively small number of Zulus in the upper echelon of the ANC. It was a time when Inkatha purported to be an internal wing of the ANC, so it was important for the ANC that Zuma be in the leadership of the ANC.'

Pillay remembers that wherever he was, Zuma would try to control the situation. 'Zuma would set up his own organisation always. Never mind he was the president of a country, he would still set up an informal apparatus. That is sort of second nature to him.'

Vawda says that the Providence unit, with different permutations of comrades, continued to meet in Swaziland from the late 1970s through to the 1980s, with Pillay and other senior ANC activists such as Zuma, Mac Maharaj and Ronnie Kasrils.

Zuma and Gordhan's revolutionary paths crossed again when the two men played crucial roles in the ANC's Operation Vula, which was active in KwaZulu-Natal in the late 1980s. Zuma, who was based outside the country, headed up the Bible Project, which was run by the Mandla Judson Kuzwayo unit and fed intelligence to the Vula high command, while Gordhan was the secretary of the operation.

◈

After democracy, Gordhan and Zuma both went into government, Gordhan as a member of the national assembly, chairing the local-government portfolio committee, and Zuma as the member of the executive committee for economic affairs and tourism in KwaZulu-Natal. When Gordhan went to SARS in 1999, Zuma was appointed deputy president of South Africa – a position he held until 2005, when then president Thabo Mbeki fired him.

Mbeki came to the conclusion that it 'would be best to release the honourable Jacob Zuma from his responsibilities as Deputy President' after the Durban high court convicted Zuma's friend and financial adviser Schabir Shaik of corruption and fraud. The court found that Shaik had paid Zuma in return for government contracts, and had solicited a bribe from French arms firm Thint Holdings to pay Zuma for his protection from any potential inquiries into the arms deal.

Testimony showed that Zuma was always short of money, and that Shaik had funded his lavish lifestyle. Judge Hillary Squires found overwhelming evidence of a corrupt relationship between the two men.

Zuma was out, but not down. He'd emerged from exile as a hard-ened political streetfighter and had no intention of seeing the inside of a court room. It was probably then that he plotted his path to the presidency. He mobilised his support, and the ANC's Youth League, Women's League, Cosatu and the SACP fell in behind him.

In 2006, he was charged with raping Fezekile Ntsukela Kuzwayo, the daughter of his friend Mandla Judson Kuzwayo, whose name was attached to the MK unit Zuma had commanded. This didn't deter his supporters, who dubbed him 'the people's president' and saw his populism as a refreshing change from the frosty and aloof Mbeki. Pro-Zuma groups wearing '100% Zuluboy' T-shirts and carrying banners with slogans such as 'Burn the Bitch' flocked to the trial. Zuma greeted them with his trademark song, 'Umshini wam' ('Bring me my machine gun').

He was acquitted in 2006 and, in an extraordinary political come-back, he dethroned Mbeki to be elected ANC president at the party's national conference in Polokwane in December 2007. Eight months later, he got his own back when Mbeki resigned after the ANC's NEC decided to 'recall' him.

The NPA then decided to withdraw the charges of corruption against Zuma, clearing his path to the country's top post.

Pillay, who had returned from exile and had become a senior executive at SARS, was hopeful when Zuma, his old struggle com-rade, was inaugurated. *Here's someone who listens*, he thought. 'The thing I liked about him is that, superficially, he's a genial guy, he doesn't have airs about him. He's approachable' says Pillay. 'Mistak-enly, I believed he knew what he knew, and he knew what he didn't know. I thought he'd be prepared to bring [in] people … that knew. The first few years [of Zuma's presidency] weren't too bad, actually. But it went south fast.'

It wasn't long before Pillay discovered that Zuma's tax affairs were in a shambles. 'I could see the writing was on the wall. I went to Pravin Gordhan and said, "Listen, at some point, Zuma is going to be under investigation. We're going to be dragged into this thing. We should get word to Zuma to get his taxes in order, because we don't want to be forced to have a look at these things and then find problems."'

Pillay went to see Zuma and explained that SARS wanted him to get his taxes sorted out. 'So from my point of view, we were managing the risks. We didn't want to get drawn into the political battles. I said to him, "Please, it must go on record that you're dealing with your issues. You must send us a letter to say you want to get your things in order." Our approach to him was the same as our approach to anybody; we come to you and say there's a problem, and it's better for us, less cost for us, less resources and less time, if you cooperate.'

SARS subscribed to a compliance model that reduced penalties to errant taxpayers if they cooperated with the authorities. 'So when it came to Zuma's tax affairs, like anybody else's, the first approach was to say, "We'll work with you to get it right, but what is owed to the fiscus is owed to the fiscus. We have no right to cut deals with anybody." We may have gone slightly more out of our way with Zuma because we didn't want to get drawn into unnecessary battles.'

But SARS did get dragged into the battle and, in fact, became an early victim of Zuma's bid to disarm his opponents. Soon after Pillay tried to negotiate a deal with Zuma, he and a number of senior SARS officials were purged from the organisation. Tom Moyane, who had been installed as commissioner in 2014, came to be seen as Zuma's hatchet man.

'The SARS model,' says one senior government official, 'is that if you are commissioner, you are God, okay, because you have all the power. And that was fine when we had someone like Pravin, who is not corrupt and works incredibly well. But then we had the worst of the worst in Moyane, and with that same power he destroyed SARS. We couldn't stop him.'

Moyane refused to acknowledge Gordhan's authority, and Zuma spurned Gordhan's request, as minister of finance, that Zuma fire the controversial tax chief for insubordination.

⊹

Africa says that because of Gordhan and Zuma's shared history in the struggle, it was painful for Gordhan to witness Zuma's descent into moral bankruptcy. Hanekom, however, says he never reflected on this as a betrayal, but rather as a challenge: How do we stop him? How do we get rid of this guy?

'I don't think at any point from any of us, really, there was a sense of betrayal. Rather, there was a sense of well, actually, now he's become the enemy, he's become the facilitator of state capture, and under his helm and with his support ... the gains of democracy are being eroded and eroded rapidly.'

What bubbled up at SARS – the much discredited 'rogue unit' and Pillay's early pension from 2010 – was a sharp thorn in Gordhan's flesh, and has been used repeatedly by his enemies against him.

Public protector Busisiwe Mkhwebane used it in an attempt to discredit him, finding against him on both issues and recommending he be 'disciplined'. Gordhan went to court to have her reports overturned, which they were – and in a scathing judgment, the Gauteng high court ruled that Mkhwebane's 'rogue unit' report was the product of 'a wholly irrational process, bereft of any sound legal or factual basis', and based on discredited reports and unsubstantiated facts. The court also found that Mkhwebane had ignored evidence and dismissed facts, and said she had approached her investigation determined to make adverse findings against Gordhan.

Moyane and Mkhwebane were just two in a succession of Zuma loyalists who launched personal attacks and smears on Gordhan. Former social development minister Bathabile Dlamini almost collapsed the social-grant payout in 2017, after which Gordhan proposed that the banks and the post office distribute social grants to the country's seventeen million beneficiaries, instead of the dubious Cash Paymaster Services. Dlamini – who the constitutional court later found had been reckless and grossly negligent – laid into Gordhan for this.

Gordhan was also targeted by forces who didn't want to see amendments to the Financial Intelligence Centre Act being passed. Zuma delayed signing the amendments – which gave authorities power to scrutinise the finances and transactions of 'politically exposed persons' – into law until litigation was launched to force him to do so.

During this political standoff while he was the finance minister, Gordhan would do his duty, and go and brief Zuma before the budget meeting and budget delivery and on important economic matters. He also encountered his boss at ANC NEC meetings. 'A simple hello,' says Gordhan. 'That's it. Oh, he can laugh and joke, no matter how much he hates you. He's quite a character. ' (Fittingly, Zuma's middle name, Gedleyihlekisa, means 'one who laughs while grinding his enemies'.)

Sandy Africa remembers Gordhan returning from meetings with Zuma and shaking his head because he'd rubbed the president up the wrong way by refusing to do something on a matter of principle.

She says all the legal battles and the never-ending saga around the so-called rogue unit were frustrating for Gordhan because they caused him to divert his attention from his work. 'I think not only did he take it hard because of the breakdown of the relationship [with Zuma], but also because of the fact that he himself became a target, and had to deal with legal issues, court appearances, engaging lawyers and just managing his life on several fronts. I suppose, over time, the relationship got more and more strained. Ja, it was hard for him,' she says.

Hanekom says the proponents of state capture wanted Gordhan out of the way but he knew what he wanted to achieve and what had to be done. 'He certainly wasn't going to just succumb and just give in to them. Indeed, he refused to budge,' says Hanekom.

Gordhan was adamant that the only way he would go would be if Zuma fired him.

In September 2016, just days before he was charged with fraud, Gordhan was asked by a reporter from the business news service Bloomberg how he was coping at the centre of the political storm. 'My spine is still very straight,' the minister replied. 'My generation are not just bureaucrats or politicians, we are activists. We continue to do that which is necessary to promote social justice as South Africa evolves in its democracy, but more importantly to stand up against injustice.'

After the charges against him were dropped a month later, Gordhan told Bloomberg that he was the victim of 'persecution and political mischief driven by rent-seekers' intent on getting their hands on the state's coffers. 'I've been in public service for forty-odd years, inside detention, outside detention, police harassment, the works. What motivates people like us, not just me but a whole lot of people who can all get better jobs, can get paid better, is public service.'

Gordhan says it was his refusal to hand over the treasury to Zuma that 'ultimately led to Mr Charming reaching a point of desperation in March 2017' and firing him. Stripped of his portfolio, Gordhan became an ordinary MP, participating in the portfolio committee on public enterprises, and becoming heavily involved in the campaign around Cyril Ramaphosa's bid for the ANC presidency. 'I was among the first to say that he would make a better president than anybody else. Some still hold that as a grudge against me ... but so be it,' he says.

Promising to get rid of the patronage and corruption that had taken root in the governing party, Ramaphosa narrowly edged out Zuma's ally, his ex-wife Nkosazana Dlamini-Zuma, at the ANC's national conference in December 2017. Zuma was forced to resign as president two months later and Ramaphosa took his place, re-appointing Gordhan to the cabinet as minister of public enterprises.

The corruption charges Zuma had spent all those years outrunning finally caught up with him, and in April 2018 he was recharged with fraud and racketeering linked to the arms deal.

It was checkmate.

'I once lived with a chess grandmaster and the most extraordinary thing was he would be making supper while he was playing three games of chess simultaneously with three different people around the world,' says Murray Michell, former director of the Financial Intelligence Centre, who met Gordhan during the UDF days in the early 1980s and has worked closely with him over the years. 'That's [Gordhan] as well, in a different scenario. He has an extraordinary mind, an extraordinary ability to see the game, and to respond.

'Pravin claims he's a lousy chess player,' says Michell. 'I don't believe him.'

16

The Burden of Competence

Only seven of the seven hundred-plus SOEs in South Africa fall under the department of public enterprises, but they're among the biggest, and include Transnet, SAA, Eskom and Denel, the aerospace and military technology conglomerate. They were also first to be targeted in the state-capture years.

So there was no small amount of irony in President Cyril Ramaphosa handing the public enterprises portfolio to Pravin Gordhan. Gordhan had, of course, become the face of resistance to state capture in the latter years of Zuma's reign. Now he was being asked to clean up the mess about which he'd been warning South Africans for many years.

The department of public enterprises exists to ensure the 'optimal economic and developmental impact' of SOEs. Its mandate includes ensuring that SOEs are financially sustainable, properly funded and 'operationally robust' – all to be done in line with national-development objectives.

When Gordhan took over, the department was ticking none of those boxes. Two of the SOEs for which his department is responsible, SAA and SA Express (a subsidiary of SAA), were in business rescue; SA Express has since been placed in provisional liquidation. A third, Eskom, was a shambles and unable to fulfil its basic mandate – to keep the country's lights on.

The scale of the task facing Gordhan was, and remains, massive. A colleague describes the job as 'a poisoned chalice' and a 'huge, huge, huge task'. Former minister Derek Hanekom says it's 'almost Mission Impossible'.

And we're still learning about the impact of the Zuma years on SOEs. In early May 2021, for example, News24's investigative team got its hands on a 'leaked trove' of Eskom documents, including letters, forensic reports, emails, bank statements and 'payment analysis'. What they discovered there was devastating: for a start, more than R178 billion of tenders awarded by the power utility in the preceding decade had been red-flagged as suspicious by investigators from the Eskom-appointed law firm Bowmans and the Special Investigative Unit (SIU), the forensic investigation and litigation agency in the department of justice. That money, News24 pointed out, would be 'enough to fully vaccinate the entire South African population with Covid-19 shots roughly twenty times over'. The comment is a reminder of who the main victims of state capture have been: South Africans who are neither rich nor connected.

The News24 investigation also revealed that Eskom had laid more than 110 complaints with the police since 2018. Eskom spokesperson Sikonathi Mantshantsha told the news site that the SIU had referred 60 cases to the NPA for prosecution and another 53 matters to the NPA's Asset Forfeiture Unit. The numbers are quite breathtaking, and another indication that the scale of looting during the state-capture years was greater than most South Africans seem to realise.

The procurement budgets in the SOEs under the department of public enterprises are significant, so it's not surprising that the state-capture vultures were circling them from early on in their project, or that the looting frenzy continued through the Zuma years. 'And the consequence of it is that there's been this massive hollowing-out of the finances, and so debt levels have just gone through the roof, and really rapidly as well,' says a department of public enterprises insider. 'So now you have a combination of things: you have financial instability, you have dysfunctionality at the operations level, [and] you have a toxic culture.'

When Gordhan took over the department, he and his senior officials anticipated that about ten percent of the staff in the SOEs would be compromised, ten percent would be good guys – whistleblowers and the like – and the other eighty percent would essentially be followers: they would align themselves with whatever direction the leadership chose. But, says the insider, 'it hasn't worked out like that because so many people are involved in this thing – it goes from top to bottom.'

Gordhan says that the rot set in towards the end of 2010 when Zuma fired Barbara Hogan as minister of public enterprises and replaced her with Malusi Gigaba, who's been facing allegations of corruption before the Zondo commission. What Gordhan describes as the 'repurposing' of the SOEs appears to have continued through Lynne Brown's subsequent tenure as minister.

'And today we've inherited all that nonsense and people have short memories about where we come from,' says Gordhan. 'So we think everything is collapsing in the Ramaphosa administration but, in fact, what we're doing now is repairing the ... damage that took place then.'

Another thing he's having to confront is inflated wage bills. 'Post-2011, Gigaba and company employed literally thousands of people in the middle areas of SOEs who had minimal skills levels and little to contribute, but who fattened the payroll,' says Gordhan.

'That was to change the employment equity numbers and outlook. Of course, we need to do that, but not in that way. That is when the cost structure of many of these entities went awry.'

Of course, Gordhan has to be mindful of the attitudes of various South African constituencies toward the future of the SOEs, an important one of which for the ANC is labour, which is dead set against closures and the consequent job losses.

Another issue is the governance structure of SOEs, which one official describes to us as 'ridiculous ... impossible'. The decision-making process is extremely cluttered, with the public enterprises minister beholden to the cabinet, which is itself beholden to the policies of the ANC, as overseen by the party's NEC.

'So there's a kind of direct line between ANC policy, firstly, as overseen by the NEC, which is then given effect by cabinet through a minister, and then through to the board and through to the executive,' the official explains. And the proliferation of SOEs and different reporting lines into various ministries makes this even more convoluted.

This scenario has also been complicated by the fact that President Ramaphosa enjoys only a slim majority in the ANC (and consequently in its NEC). This, a party member observes, means that every decision taken to that body 'is on a tightrope and subject to political pressure and contestation'.

Gordhan drily points out that the narrative shaped by the South African 'mode of thinking' is that decisions are ascribed to individuals. 'I'm a member of the cabinet. I'm a member of the ANC NEC. I'm a member of the government. I can't decide on my own whether I'm going to save something or get money for something or take something in a particular direction. There are processes that are there that we have to go through. And you must get approval for those processes. You don't just go and shoot ahead ...'

An official points out that all this needs to be addressed in broader economic circumstances that are less than ideal: 'There is simply no more money.'

So what can be done?

Nothing specific had been documented in terms of a strategy at the time of writing, but Gordhan does point to the work of Mariana Mazzucato, an economist who's a professor at University College London in the economics of innovation and public value, and is the founder and director of the university's Institute for Innovation and Public Purpose.

In 2021 Mazzucato, her institute colleague Rainer Kattel and Wits's Mzukisi Qobo published a paper called 'Building state capacities and dynamic capabilities to drive social and economic development: The case of South Africa'. The paper's scope reaches across the entire state, but it does address the roles that the authors envisage SOEs playing in South Africa.

On the broad issue of the state's role in an economy, the authors contemplate 'a different notion of the state – not just a market fixer but also a market co-creator and shaper'. They add, 'Our approach is not about more state or less state, but a different type of state: one that is characterised by innovative institutions, embodies public value and is able to act as an investor of first resort, catalysing new types of growth and in so doing crowd in private-sector investment and innovation.'

Turning to SOEs, they point out that recent failures have led 'many to question whether the state should hold on to these, with suggestions that these should be privatised'. 'In our view, the question is not whether SOEs should exist or not. What is of utmost importance is how their missions are defined and how they operate as constituent parts of a mixed economic system, where the state has an opportunity to co-create markets and provide the social and economic infrastructure that would otherwise not be supplied by the private sector.'

They stress the importance of 'building partnerships across various social sectors' and suggest that in the case of SOEs this 'may entail taking a lead in supplying critical public infrastructure or services, especially in areas where the private sector would not invest on its own'.

Gordhan says, somewhat grumpily, that South Africa's business sector and the commentariat occupy 'a very conservative neoliberal mould', 'so the narratives are all painted within that kind of framework'. But 'as the world has moved on', and with the impact of Covid-19, thinking about the economy and its impact on people's lives has become 'completely different'.

This applies, for example, to the way benefits accrue to the elite, health systems, welfare systems and 'the extent to which countries have had to provide stimulus packages even at the expense of debt-to-GDP [gross domestic product] ratios and so on' to make sure that lives and livelihoods are saved. Governments traditionally aim to keep debt-to-GDP ratios low in order to be able to manage debt without incurring further debt. 'So there's a whole new paradigm, in that sense, and that applies equally to state-owned entities. If you look at the global picture, state-owned entities have become even more dominant, in both the so-called West and East.'

Gordhan points to China's State-owned Assets Supervision and Administration Commission and Singapore's Temasek, and the fact that in France SOEs contribute significantly to the country's GDP: 'And yet you think France is a capitalist country.'

He also cites the USA's Defense Advanced Research Projects Agency, whose website explains that it invests in what it calls 'breakthrough technologies for national security' and which has also developed game-changing 'icons of modern civilian society such as the internet, automated voice recognition and language translation, and global positioning system (GPS) receivers small enough to embed in myriad consumer devices'.

In their paper, Mazzucato, Qobo and Kattel refer to the Norwegian model, where 'the shareholding structure of government is diffused across 11 government departments, with state equity ranging between 30 percent and 100 percent. Apart from the government pension fund of Norway and the well-known Statoil in the gas and oil sector, Norway commands 70 other SOEs spanning aerospace, health, local government, banking, arts and culture, genetic seed breeding, construction and civil engineering services, coal mining, property development, fibre optics and mobile telephony, among others.'

So what might all this mean in the South African context?

Ramaphosa is engaging directly with the issue, and in 2020 launched the Presidential State-Owned Enterprises Council, which he chairs but in which Gordhan plays a central role.

According to a statement from the presidency, 'the council has been tasked by the president to advise government on the repositioning of SOEs, development of appropriate governance frameworks; to identify specific interventions to stabilise and strengthen SOEs' financial and operational performance and reduce reliance on the fiscus, and ensure SOEs are repurposed to align with national priorities'. An obvious benefit of this approach is that it skirts the governance issues, effectively putting oversight into the hands of one body.

'We are in the process of ... evaluating all of the SOEs, big and small, and working out which are the critical ones, which need to be either shut down or consolidated, or whatever the case might be,' says Gordhan. 'It'll take us a couple of months to get there. Lots of people are going to be uncomfortable at the end of that, but that's where we're heading. So that's the broader trajectory, as a state, that we're following.'

Ramaphosa said in his February 2019 state of the nation address, 'Where SOEs are not able to raise sufficient financing from banks, from capital markets, from development finance institutions or from the fiscus, we will need to explore other mechanisms, such as strategic equity partnerships or selling off non-strategic assets.'

A government insider familiar with the process says Ramaphosa's comments have given rise to 'serious questions being asked and grappled with'. For example, are all South Africa's seven hundred-plus SOEs necessary or do they need to be 'whittled down'? 'Perhaps those that remain will be those that are considered "strategic" and have to be functioning more cohesively as a state-owned body, on the basis of a different model, along the lines of those in Singapore or in China,' says the insider, who speculates that in ten years' time there may only be about fifteen large SOEs. 'And then there's all the rest: does the state need to own them? Why do they need to be there? Should they not be closed down, disposed of, etcetera?'

She points to the structure of a large company with subsidiaries as an example for the state-SOE relationship. In this case, the state would be the 'holding company' and the subsidiaries – the remaining SOEs – have got to function efficiently. On the one hand, they may be required to yield a dividend to the shareholders, and then they've got to be able to hit their targets. On the other hand, they may be asked to provide essential services 'for the public good, in which case they will need to be supported'. 'But either way, they need to be contributing to and adding to the development of the economy, for the benefit of the country as a whole.'

Another part of the process will be 'to unpack each of those SOEs in the restructuring process, to say, "How do you manage them singly – as an entity – but also as a group? Do you need to strip them of core versus non-core, and then do something different with the non-core stuff?"' she says.

For example, some of the SOEs own considerable amounts of property across the country. Is it going to be needed for future strategic purposes? Do some need the huge offices they currently have? In a future South Africa where the economy is picking up, might Denel not be able to develop technology in a similar fashion to the USA's Defense Advanced Research Projects Agency? Or turn its attention to other issues, such as water and climate, which could have an impact on security?

Perhaps the thorniest issue that has faced Gordhan in the SOE space is that of SAA, devastated by mismanagement over many years and the subject of controversial multibillion-rand bailouts. The *Mail & Guardian* calculated that 'with the R10,5-billion bailout allocated to SAA [in 2020], the airline has received more than R60 billion in government guarantees'.

An insider said the anger over the bailing-out of SAA was understandable but that shutting it down would be akin to 'throwing the baby out with the bathwater' and that there's still value in the airline. The impact on the aviation sector as a whole in South Africa should also be taken into account.

He speculates that SAA might, for example, re-emerge as an airline with a significant capacity for ferrying cargo, particularly across the African continent. 'If you leave it to the market, they're going to go for where they can make the most profits in the short term and they're going to leave these huge gaps, which might not be as lucrative, but are still absolutely necessary for the regional economy and social wellbeing.'

Mcebisi Jonas reacted to criticism of the SAA bailout by calling Gordhan and asking for a meeting. He started the discussion by asking Gordhan, 'Don't you think you're pushing it too hard?'

He recalls leaving the discussion 'smiling' after Gordhan had explained his approach. 'Maybe the solution is transforming some of the state-owned enterprises to become real companies, in the sense of looking at the bottom line and better management and so on, like in Malaysia and Singapore,' says Jonas.

A South Africa-based analyst suggests that the SAA bailouts might be the consequence of a 'trade-off' behind the scenes, the substance of which might only become evident in time.

✦

In the second week of June 2021, two significant announcements were made that suggested decisive movement in the SOE space.

On 11 June 2021 – as this book was going to press – Gordhan announced that the government was selling a 51-percent stake in SAA to a private equity partner, the Takatso consortium, which news agency Reuters reported would 'initially commit more than 3 billion rand ($221,60 million) to give the struggling airline a new lease of life'. The department of public enterprises will own the other 49 percent.

Speaking at a press conference to announce the partnership, Gordhan said the deal meant that the state would no longer provide any funding to the airline.

The deal was announced weeks after the airline emerged from a sixteen-month-long business-rescue process. *Business Day* newspaper reported that 'that process allowed it to leave behind its hefty financial baggage – employee costs and debt repayments – to allow turnaround specialists to slim it down, dress it up for an equity partner and wean it off government bailouts'.

Earlier in the week Ramaphosa had announced that private entities would be able to generate electricity up to 100MW for their own needs and to sell on without a licence. *Business Day* columnist Carol Paton described this development as 'huge' and 'the single biggest microeconomic reform in years'; it will, she wrote, 'change the electricity market, as we have always known it, forever'.

The SAA deal, she added, was the 'cherry on the top' and 'the government has run well ahead of where the ANC stands on privatisation'.

Interestingly, the ANC caucus in parliament issued a statement welcoming both developments.

✦

There are holdouts, the National Union of Metalworkers of South Africa and the South African Federation of Trade Unions among them. There has also been criticism from opposition parties and the so-called RET forces aligned to Jacob Zuma. These aren't insignificant and Gordhan still has major challenges with Eskom and the other SOEs that fall under his portfolio. He remains in a difficult and unenviable position.

But, as Peter Richer said of him in an interview before the SAA deal was announced, 'You always knew that he was coming from a position of wanting to do the best for the country. It was never about doing the best for Pravin Gordhan. One might disagree with the decisions he makes – I mean, right now, I can't understand for the life of me what the hell's going on with SAA – but you can bet that it has nothing to do with Pravin Gordhan's self-interest. It only has to do with what Pravin Gordhan thinks is best for the country.'

17

'Do not waste one minute of his life'

Derek Hanekom remembers taking a call from Yunus Shaik when South Africa had gone into the Covid-19 lockdown of 2020. Yunus is one of the six Shaik brothers and in the struggle years was an underground operative alongside Pravin Gordhan. Now he had a business interest in the tourism industry and 'some of the measures didn't make sense to him'.

Hanekom, a former tourism minister who was by 2020 a presidential envoy tasked with promoting investment, responded, 'Well, I can speak to one or two people but I'm not in cabinet. Maybe you should speak to Pravin, since you've known each other for so long?'

'And Yunus said, "No. I can speak to you but I can't speak to Pravin. Pravin was my commander ... speaking to Pravin is like speaking to God."'

Hanekom laughs: 'A lot of people hold him in this very high regard.'

Others are, of course, less complimentary. The most outspoken are the state-capture looters and the RET crowd, who see him as their

205

bête noire and have directed outlandish and often nonsensical slurs in his direction.

But some of his erstwhile contemporaries also point out that he's not entirely flawless.

So what sort of person is Pravin Gordhan?

The public persona is easiest to discern. From his early struggle days he showed a gift for organisation and strategic thinking. This, combined with a willingness to work hard, made him a formidable and influential activist.

Mpho Scott remembers Gordhan as 'a born strategist ... Pravin was gifted in terms of how you look at a problem, what you need [to address it] and what you can do.'

Ivan Pillay says Gordhan 'always struck me as being meticulous about organisation'. 'During the years of the underground it was clear that he was somebody who was prepared to dirty his hands, really get involved. He had a reputation which I knew of from outside [the country] of being very strong, very focused.'

Mcebisi Jonas was a younger activist in the then Natal. 'At the time he really was a very good, solid theoretician. And [that] was very important for us youngsters and for me, because reflection on some of these things is important,' says Jonas. 'But he also had a rare combination of being a theoretician and also a strategist.'

Moe Shaik says Gordhan 'mastered the art and the science of organisation'.

Yousuf Vawda remembers, 'Pravin's qualities came through very strongly – his sharp intellect and his ability to absorb a whole lot of information and process it and respond effectively in situations. He understood the organisational sense and mass orientation better than most, and was able to drive things. And then something that has come up over and over again is his strategic sense; he has a very keen strategic sense. He gets an idea very quickly of what the situation is, what the options are that are available, and what the optimal option to go for is.'

Derek Hanekom concurs: 'He's the best strategic thinker that I've ever come across, ever,' he says.

So was he all work and no play? Abba Omar says, 'I think he was kind of culturally aware of movies and novels and that kind of thing.' They rarely chatted about such things 'but I know he'd able to reference them quite easily'. 'But activism was, like, 99.99 percent of Pravin's life. Babs, my brother, would say he felt like he was reading a textbook every time he would be sitting with Pravin. I liked it. Some people are like that, and I used to enjoy it.'

'He can be wonderfully charming, although his life is not one of being on a charm offensive – he's not garrulous, he's not a racon-teur,' says a colleague. 'He's straight to the point.' He might respond to 'resistance' in meetings with a sarcastic comment, 'so that some-times pees people off'. 'And yet at the same time, he's unbelievably warm and he's got an amazing sense of humour. So when he's in a safe space and he's allowed to laugh, then …'

Sandy Africa saw a 'kind of generosity' in Gordhan's decision to set up a pharmacy and effectively use it as a front after he'd been fired from King Edward VIII Hospital. The business of the pharmacy took second place to the activist meetings it hosted. It also became a place where secret messages were routinely dropped and picked up by activists.

✦

As his profile grew, and he was detained and tortured, 'That wasn't going to deter him,' says Vidhu Vedalankar. 'That's what we knew of him.'

Pillay says, 'He is very, very careful about his own reputation, very careful about the ethics of anything that he does, and he's likely to check and counter-check those things until people have given him a level of confidence.'

Mandla Nkomfe has had a long association with Gordhan, from when he was a student activist in Gauteng. 'I must tell you that nothing has changed. The empowering presence that he has – and when you think something is very, very difficult he makes it quite easy for you to understand and really lifts you up,' he says. 'I think his strategic focus is still there, that organisational sense is there, and, really, his presence, his level of presence in whatever endeavour that he gets involved in or engaged with.'

Murray Michell, a long-standing struggle colleague who's worked with Gordhan in government for many years, describes his approach to meetings: 'He's a meticulous note taker. Everything is recorded and everything is kept [stored] and you reference back to it. So there's a constant subconscious fact-checking, which he will then always triangulate with other references so he knows what's going down all the time.'

Gordhan also insists on meticulous note keeping by others: 'a constant writing up' of events, says another colleague. 'So if you're engaged in a particular area of work, it will be written up on a day-by-day basis, and so as you move into day two, you've got day one recorded; move into day three, you've got days one and two recorded. It's an extraordinary approach, but it means there's a constant reference, so when it gets to a point where you're putting together a speech or a presentation, the record is there.

'The other [thing is that] he tests ideas all the time. He'll test hypotheses, he'll test ideas, and then if they're correct, [they] will be acted upon. If there's a negative, then they'll be discarded. So it's almost a scientific approach to dealing with this.'

This testing is sometimes done through role playing: 'He'll put two or three people in the room and say, "Right, you are so-and-so, you are so-and-so," and say, "What questions are you going to ask me if I fire this at you, how are you going to respond?" and you will put it on the table and have an argy-bargy,' says the colleague. 'It's that meticulous and thorough: looking at things from all angles, trying to anticipate and understand where somebody else or the other side is going to come from, what the arguments are going to be, what facts they're likely to put on the table, how you're going to rebut it, how you're going to deal with it, manage it.'

Johann van Loggerenberg, who worked for Gordhan at SARS, says, 'He's the sort of guy you want to prepare for because you're going to get taken out if you don't prepare. So you prepare, and you prepare, and you rehearse and you, like, really give it your all. And then you also go and ask other people to help you to just pressure-test this thing, so that when you walk in there you're ready for him.

'And it's not fear – it's fear of disappointing. You're not scared of Pravin Gordhan, you're scared of not living up to his view of how human beings should be, particularly in South Africa. So you walk in there and you feel amped, and then he has this ability to take you into the big picture if you go into the detail, and when you go into the big picture he takes you down to the detail. And so that's how you prepare.'

And how does he react if somebody hasn't prepared adequately?

A former colleague reacts with a laugh: 'Ja, you've seen these graphics from the Middle Ages …'

Somebody will leave with their head on a spike?

'Exactly. You'll get embarrassed the first time round and you'll be tackled and you need to be able to explain yourself. If you can't, you have a serious problem, but don't dare come back a second time unprepared – you'll just get thrown out of the meeting. So lots of people who aren't able to keep up or deliver will just be put in the naughty corner, and that's the end of it. There's no relationship after that. So that's where people get terrified.'

Gordhan will be 'utterly fair' but 'if you can't deliver then you're not worth sitting at the table'.

On the flip side, there are people he's worked with whom he 'doesn't necessarily know or doesn't necessarily particularly like' who are given a seat at the table because they do deliver.

Many interviewees described Gordhan as 'complex', and by several accounts there are contradictory elements to his personality. For example, in spite of evidently being stubborn, he is prepared to change his mind. Vawda, reminiscing about their struggle days, says, 'He had intellectual rigour, but he wasn't dogmatic. He had a point of view and pushed it and fought very hard for his position. And if you wanted to change his mind, you had to have a damn good argument and be able to push it and persevere.'

A current colleague who's worked alongside Gordhan for several years says, 'Oh, ja, he has a hypothesis [but] it's not a preconceived, definitive notion, necessarily. He recognises he's not always right.'

Nkomfe says he can be persuaded that his position is wrong. 'So you'll come with an idea, but you'll all workshop this idea in a very robust way, and by the time you finish, he would have changed his mind.'

Hanekom agrees. 'It's not a problem, but you have to have a strong case before you can change his mind on anything.'

A colleague says Gordhan is big on trust: 'He needs to know he's working with persons he can trust. He expects they're treating information as confidential, understanding what to do with it, what not to do with it.'

Ethics and principles, says Jonas, are central to Gordhan's modus operandi. In spite of this, opponents have repeatedly tried to portray him as venal, but it's not an allegation that finds any purchase with the people who know him well.

Pillay says: 'There isn't a corrupt bone in Pravin's body. In that way, he's completely selfless. As a person involved in administration, he was very clear about the fact that we are accountable … we must want to account, which sets him apart from other people: it's not about somebody making you account, it's about you wanting to account.'

Vawda says the EFF's allegations about Gordhan being corrupt 'cannot stick'. 'I mean, he is unimpeachable on that level. Not that he doesn't have personal flaws, but on that score there is no question about it.'

One of his oldest struggle colleagues says, 'Pravin is very committed to the fight against corruption and is certainly not corrupt. I would know that he wouldn't take a cent from anybody. He's got integrity.'

Judge Dennis Davis has been friends with Gordhan for some thirty years. 'He's got a real moral compass and that drives him,' he says. He believes that Gordhan found his clash with Zuma 'incongruous' but 'he saw the sheer horror of what Zuma was up to and he took on the role'. 'I was with him when people would come up to him and tell him that he's doing what Nelson Mandela did, and he would tell them, "Don't be silly, Mandela was in a totally different class to me". He was embarrassed that he was getting all this acclaim at the time. That wasn't his nature. But he is like Mandela in the sense that he doesn't see colour; he sees principle – in a world where there are very few people like that.'

⯎

Mcebisi Jonas says, 'PG was very hard on performance, he was very hard on delivery, he was very hard on work. If you want, he's a kind of a nice, good, solid slavedriver … but if you're lazy, you have problems with PG. And if you're stupid, you have problems.' He laughs. 'He doesn't suffer fools. Also, if you're unprincipled, you're in trouble.'

Van Loggerenberg adds, 'He wasn't somebody that I experienced as making small talk, or wasting time, or making jokes, or being playful or that kind of thing. I always experienced him as very determined, very clear, very driven, and very, very, very serious. And don't waste his time. Do not waste one minute of his life. He was a hard, hard taskmaster, but he had a vision. In the instances where I interacted with him, he was business only and he would not suffer fools.'

Nkomfe says that Gordhan will quickly see when somebody is 'bullshitting' and doesn't take kindly to it. 'He tells you straight. He has no time for niceties.' Nkomfe believes that accusations of arrogance levelled against Gordhan come from this trait.

Vawda recalls similar perceptions from the earlier struggle days: 'He has a quite strong personality and could be very dominant in discussions in meetings because I think he was generally a couple of steps ahead of most people. This could be perceived as being domineering, and sometimes intimidating, and that was an area where we had occasion to give some feedback and he was able to take that and deal with it.'

A former cabinet minister with a long-standing association with Gordhan says 'there are a number of reports of people who say that he has been very harsh and disciplinarian, to the point of being rude with people'.

One former struggle colleague says pointedly, 'Obviously, [he's] a great guy, [with] a lot of humility, but it's occasional sort of stuff that I think you need to keep in mind. I mean, he is no angel – there are aspects to him that are on the dark side as well.'

He believes Gordhan is 'very aware of how he's seen, wants to be liked and that kind of thing', and this results in him demanding absolute loyalty from people. This, he says, has given rise to fallouts with at least two prominent comrades who Gordhan believed were associating with an individual whom he saw as an enemy.

He acknowledges Gordhan has a 'really brilliant mind' but is wary of his 'wanting to be acknowledged, appreciated, etcetera … and an expectation of loyalty'.

◈

Gordhan has been accused by enemies of arrogance and being egotistical, and one of his former struggle colleagues says that while he's genuinely humble, there are people who 'wear their humility loudly'.

In interviews for this book, however, the authors found Gordhan extremely reluctant to take credit for many of the things people attributed to him, from his role in conceptualising mass mobilisation to helping create the UDF, being central to the crafting of a new constitution, the success at SARS, standing up to Jacob Zuma and the state-capture looters, and much more.

In nearly eight hours of interviews he gave us, there were just two occasions where he gave himself credit. The first was for pioneering the struggle concept of OCMS – organisation, consciousness, mobilisation, struggle – of which he seems particularly proud, and in which others happily acknowledge his role.

The other was for being able to manage at a strategic level and also get into operational detail. He made the latter comment after being asked about allegations that he's a micromanager, and immediately qualified it by saying, 'It's a terrible thing to say about oneself …'

He's bluntly unapologetic about his management style, and appears to have given it some thought. 'I can't tell you what Ivan Pillay did from day to day [in SARS], what the enforcement guys did every day in terms of cigarette smuggling, or whatever the case might be. So I don't micromanage at that level but, as part of my own personal learning and knowledge, I would walk the floor. Every good chief executive does that, by the way – you walk the floor so that you don't rely on three layers of managers to tell you what's going on on the ground.

'And in that way, in the tax context, you learn a hell of a lot more by talking to X because he's actually doing the PAYE work, he sees the forms, he sees the scams the tax advisers are pulling off. And I enjoy listening to that sort of stuff, because it helps you to develop a macro-strategy. You can't develop a macro-strategy from the stratosphere. It's got to be rooted in what you actually do. So I loved talking to a VAT auditor, for example, because they're the ones who go out, they're the ones who check books, they're the ones who know what kind of export scams [are going on].

'So I don't think I'd call myself a micromanager, but if you want me to get into details, I'll take you there. And the way I take you there is not by saying, "I know." I'll just keep asking you: Why? What? How? Give me the detail. Give me the rationale. But you are going to answer the question, not me.'

He stresses that it's important to test whether officials are giving him correct information. 'Otherwise, you're like a mutt sitting at the top. You're going to sign off on documents that decide on what you need to get delivered, but which are developed by officials who themselves don't have a full command of what's going on. So when the time is available, it's fascinating to get into that detail.'

He acknowledges that he sometimes puts people on the back foot by testing a proposition thoroughly, but adds that it's a part of a process of working out 'whether you know what you're talking about or not'. 'So then I think people say, "Oh, I'm scared, because [he's] going to ask me something and I'm not going to be able to explain," but if you want to come with a proposition, you'd better be able to explain it. Simple.

'In the end, it also actually improves the other person: they must become more knowledgeable, they must read more, they must organise their own day-to-day experiences in a way in which they can explain themselves. So there's a positive side to it as well. And that's how people grow.'

⬧

Gordhan's public life has been characterised by fighting – against apartheid and, more recently, corruption. 'Courage' and 'bravery' are words that are frequently used to describe him in these contexts.

Hanekom says: 'Pravin is incredibly brave. If he doesn't raise an issue in cabinet or in any other forum, it's for tactical purposes, not because he's afraid. The moment he has to speak, he's totally unafraid. He does it very effectively, and treads on a lot of toes in the process, because he's not going to water down what he says in order to be diplomatic. He doesn't use unnecessarily offensive and aggressive language, but he says what has to be said.'

'He's withstood massive, massive assaults in various forms,' says a long-standing colleague. 'He's unbelievably stubborn and principled in the face of these. Unbelievable. And his family sometimes takes immense strain because of it … He just won't step back, and it impacts on everything.'

Van Loggerenberg adds, 'I'm amazed that he's held on. I mean, he must be so tough [to have] held on for so long, because why wouldn't you just walk away from all this? Why? It's superhuman. The abuse this man has taken. Never mind the security branch ripping his beard from his face. I mean, can you imagine that?'

Nkomfe says, 'He's strong. He just closes everything and focuses, and everything else is filtered out of his mind so that he's able to move forward. And it's not easy. It's a tough one. He came through, but it's not over, not by any stretch of the imagination.'

Given the sort of focus he exerts, the demands he puts on people and the charges of aloofness and arrogance, it might be surprising that Gordhan is roundly praised for his warmth and empathy. Shamim Meer remembers Gordhan the activist as being 'highly disciplined and very caring'. 'There was a lot of caring if any one of these activists was having any problems or crises of a financial or whatever nature. That care stood out.'

An adviser to Gordhan in the department of public enterprises says 'he's incredibly caring and it shows in different ways'; he's always 'very concerned' about the wellbeing and health of his family and friends. The adviser has a medical condition and Gordhan will often ask about his health: when he last saw a doctor and what medication he's on. Then Gordhan the pharmacist kicks in: 'What did he give you? Let me have a look around for something better. No, why is he giving you this? There's a newer medicine, you can do this, you can do that.'

'But I've also noticed it with staff. They'll sometimes be asked to work long hours – sometimes 24-hour shifts, make no bones about it – but if somebody has to take the day off, it's, "Yes, you must spend time with your child, you must spend time with your family." If there's any sort of illness being shown at all, "Sort it out." So he's got a very, very strong sense of the importance of that. It's a very nice side of him.'

Hanekom adds, 'During this very difficult period, he still has time for the little things, like just checking up on a person to say, "How are you?" He visited me twice when I was in hospital with malaria.' When Hanekom's wife Trish became ill, he was on the phone to her immediately, says Hanekom. 'He is an extremely loyal person.'

'You must be with him to understand the empathy that he has, and the humanity that he has. It's outstanding,' says Nkomfe. 'Maybe he is shy, but whatever he does, he's a mentor and he's a teacher in my eyes. He's not a politician – he's a community worker, he's a revolutionary.'

✦

Gordhan's wife, family and friends have evidently been central to that strength. 'I don't think it would have been possible for him to cope with all that pressure if he was on his own and didn't have people stand with him whom he trusted and whose friendship he valued,' says Hanekom. 'It's not just a few of us who happen to have been in cabinet with him – he has wide respect in society.'

Sandy Africa, who worked briefly alongside Gordhan in the treasury in 2012 and 2013, got a 'sense of how very much of a family person, he was … very committed to his family and his wife, Vani, who I also knew as an activist, and his daughters. So I just got a sense that he was a person very grounded and rooted in his community and family, and very respected also in that context.

'And, yeah, one almost hoped that he would be someone who was a bit more flawed,' she laughs, 'but I suspect it was just because he has been so consumed by politics. I don't by any means see him as a one-dimensional person, but certainly a person who has been very much a political animal. I don't think that's all that there is to him, but that certainly has been a part of his identity.'

Beyond the public persona, Gordhan appears by choice to live an uncluttered life. 'He's a person who has lived his life simply; he's humble,' says Vedalankar. 'He doesn't have the material trimmings that you see many politicians have. And that is [a] commitment to not needing big things, not needing a lot of things in his life, and also to leading by example.'

Pillay, reflecting on their time together at SARS, says, 'He wasn't distracted by all sorts of other things. He lived a fairly simple life. And by the way, you have to – you've got to live an uncluttered life to enable you to do those things. So there was a razor-like focus.'

What might he do in his down time?

According to Nkomfe, there isn't really such a thing in Gordhan's life. 'I mean, [I] get [messages] at 1am about something that he's reading in the *Guardian*, or something; this man is still awake, still reading some stuff. So he's very active, his mind is in overdrive all the time.'

Vedalankar says, 'He's the kind of person who will always be involved in doing something that keeps his mind active, and that keeps him going. And that is why even at this age he is still in the cabinet. We would encourage him to spend more time with his family and do other things, but if he's asked [to do something] by the movement, he'll do it.' But, she adds, 'What he loves to do when he is relaxing is to spend time with his family. He loves watching sport, all kinds of sports. He likes movies. And he loves reading. He reads across a range of things, which always gives him ideas. And he picks up on different ideas that he builds on and incorporates into whatever work he's doing.'

Nkomfe says, 'He's a very private person. He's got what we say in the township is "a very strong government at home". Vani is very strict and she tries to get him to relax and slow things down.'

18

The Strong Government

Before Vanitha 'Vani' Raju became Pravin Gordhan's 'very strong government at home', she was an activist in her own right. She joined the civic organisation in the Asherville/Overport area of Natal in the 1970s and was a member of the NIC.

'We mostly disseminated literature,' she says. 'We were pamphlet pushers, and our activities were focused on trying to conscientise the community by impressing on them that our rights were being trampled on.'

Vani admits to being starstruck when she first encountered Gordhan, who was then on the NIC executive and a senior figure in the underground. 'There was all this hush-hush talk and here I was meeting a real live activist. I was in awe.'

What she came to learn about her husband – and what she says about him to this day – is that he was 'actually just very ordinary,' and that although he comes across as confident, he's 'very shy and a big softy'. 'He does a lot of second-guessing and there's an element of insecurity,' she says.

The two connected politically and, because he was a pharmacist and she a radiographer, professionally. It was only many years later, though, that they hit it off romantically. They got married when Gordhan was in hiding in 1987, but the formal recognition of the marriage had to wait until 1990, after Gordhan was released from detention.

'We were harassed by the security police,' she recalls. 'Looking over our shoulder and checking the number plates of cars behind us became a fact of life. It made us angry. All the injustice made us angry and that indignation spurred us on during the apartheid years.'

When Gordhan was detained, Vani was picked up by the security police and questioned. She pretended to be 'this naive woman who didn't know what the hell was going on'. They believed her and let her go.

Vani is still in touch with some of their former comrades from that era. 'The honesty, the integrity and the camaraderie at that time … you could take your life and put it in somebody's hand and you would know that they would look after it. It gives me goose-bumps when I think of the kind of connection that existed among us,' she says. 'People sat in discussions and debated and developed ideas, and it was all about advancing the struggle. It was a beautiful period where people developed and learned to think. It wasn't about the individual, it was the collective that contributed to ideas and decisions. When Pravin talks about his history, he talks about "us"; he never ever speaks about "I".'

According to Vani, the activists were idealistic and revered the leaders – 'even Jacob Zuma'. 'They were our heroes … and then you come up close and you see all the warts and you become disenchanted. It's heartbreaking.'

Vani never thought that one day she would be married to a cabinet minister because, she says, she and Gordhan were 'very, very ordinary people'. 'We still are,' she adds. 'We lead ordinary lives and sometimes we look at each other and ask, "So, how did we get here?"'

She can plot that trajectory but what she can't fathom is that all these years after apartheid she still has to worry about her husband's safety. 'We came through the difficult times during apartheid, which we got used to, and it's almost inconceivable that there are these attacks now in our democracy. I mean, in 2016 I thought somebody would take him out, you know. I was worried that somebody would just come and kill him.'

She says Gordhan continues with his task because he's 'tough, resilient and single-minded about the national interest'. 'It consumes him. It would be nice if we didn't have all these sideshows so that he could get on with that which he has to do.'

Gordhan certainly has a side that the public rarely sees. 'The EFF accuse him of being a bully but he's actually really soft,' says Vani. And she adds that he's not afraid to cry – but it's not out of sadness. 'Seeing people overcoming their own difficulties makes him cry.'

The Gordhans have thought about the R-word – his retirement. 'We talk about it. It's been on the agenda for a while, but there's never been the right time. At the end of his first term as finance minister, we talked about whether it was time to throw in the towel because of his age, but Pravin decided he wasn't going to rock the boat. It was an election year and he didn't want to do anything that could affect the ANC's chances, so he made himself available [to be reappointed].

'Then he was made minister of cooperative governance and traditional affairs and he decided he would pull out after the local government elections in 2016. But then he was asked to go back to the department of finance. And then there was all the harassment, and the more Zuma tried to put pressure on Pravin to leave, the more determined he was to stay.

'When the new administration came in, with all the difficulties of state capture and the institutions being hollowed out, he felt he needed to stay. So it was just never the right time to go.'

When Gordhan does eventually retire, the couple plan to spend more time indulging their non-political passions: watching cricket and tennis.

19

'Optimism is certainly there'

Pravin Gordhan's image comes into focus on the Zoom call. There are no signs of the deep furrows and worried frowns of the past few years; there's just a broad smile.

Before he logged onto Zoom he was listening to 'Guantanamera', a Spanish song inspired by a poem by José Martí, from the point of view of a Cuban revolutionary about a girl from Guantanamo. It had reminded him of a quote by Martí about empowering people through learning.

'Empowering people through learning' is precisely how Gordhan plans to spend his days when he retires (he may learn to play the piano too – a colleague told him that playing the piano for an hour before going to sleep keeps the mind agile). When he leaves office, he plans to read more and engage more in intellectual discourse to better understand different aspects of the world and society.

'No one can ever be satisfied that one "knows it all". My life has been about learning and growing and adapting through the learning. I'll have to retire at some stage from formal politics and yet look for other ways, within my ability and health, of contributing. You can retire from a job, but you can't retire as an activist,' he says.

Gordhan says he'd like to be remembered as 'just this activist who grew up on the streets of central Durban, who had the opportunity to contribute as a lifelong activist, to build the changing South Africa, but also to build the institutions of democracy – as one small contribution among many, many, many others.'

And how does he think he'll actually be remembered?

'Well, that depends on how you write the book,' he laughs, and then becomes serious. 'Actually, I think that will vary depending on what happens to the rest of my life. For the last eighteen months I've taken a lot of knocks for doing what we had to do, in respect of SAA, for example. From an anti-corruption figure, I then suddenly became stupid.'

When he retires he certainly won't miss the scornful comments and slurs directed at him. He's able to brush off the attacks about ninety percent of the time, but the barbs can hurt. 'I'm a human being and I do have feelings,' he says.

His family helps him reach a point of equanimity in relation to the insults and they encourage him to be tactical – like not responding to the EFF's dog whistles. However, in other situations he'll say what he wants to say about corrupt individuals. 'You've got to draw the balance, depending on the forum, between keeping quiet, and being quite clear that you're intolerant of corruption and malfeasance and of people associated with that. So, for me, and I'm sure for many others, your gut churns when you hear of what X or Y is doing. To use a colloquialism, it pisses you off that people who have a particular public narrative are privately engaging in all sorts of terrible stuff. That's where politics has changed from an activist orientation to, let's call it, a career orientation, where you would do anything to advance your ambition.'

He says 'the greed factor' has seen some of the heroes of the struggle succumb to corruption. 'Greed is a huge driver, and has been throughout human existence – the need to acquire something, and then the continuous need to acquire more and more, and not being so embedded in whatever values you once had as to be able to resist that urge and not to abuse the access that you have to resources. The current system, the capitalist system, in its crude form [and the idea of] keeping up with the Joneses [has caused] many people to mimic others who they got to know in business circles ... the whisky, the cigars, the lifestyle.'

The Zondo commission has heard a great deal of testimony about the tangled web of corruption that became endemic during Jacob Zuma's presidency, and Gordhan hopes the commission will produce a number of outcomes. 'The first thing, I suppose, is whether the hypothesis of state capture which we've painted for ourselves in South Africa through the academics – and it was part of my evidence in November 2019 – is a valid one. That would mean that the commission should give us an insight into how democracies like ours, and economies like ours, and states like ours, can be captured and repurposed to serve a very small group of people.'

Another outcome he'd like to see is for the commission to paint an adequate picture of what happened in some of the key institutions like Eskom, Transnet, SAA and the law-enforcement agencies, so that it becomes 'a bequeathal to future generations'. In other words, providing a roadmap of the things that the next crop of leaders have to avoid doing so they don't go down the state-capture road.

A third outcome Gordhan would like to see is for the commission to help South Africans understand the mechanisms by which the corruption happened. 'Too much of the focus in the narratives is around money. If you talk to me and my colleagues about our experience in these SOEs, it's not just money. They destroyed culture, they destroyed people, they chased away good professionals, they destroyed systems, and they destroyed values. So you actually end up with a completely corrupted entity.'

He likens the corruption to a laptop being infected with a virus. 'It's not just that you can't type the letter "W" because the key is broken. It's holistic damage that is actually created and reconstructed, and then these institutions are re-repurposed. I don't think it has been adequately understood yet. So we battle along every day, with each of these entities and the traumas that they give us. But very few people in the media have actually written about the innards. Too much of the focus is on criticising you because you're a leader, you didn't do X or Y. Too little of the focus is on actually understanding the fifty parts of a machine that are broken, and which need to be either refurbished or replaced or re-engineered in some way in order for the machine to work again. So it's the mechanisms by which all of those things have happened.'

Finally, he says, the commission should reveal who the actors were and what criminality was engaged in by these people, which could then lead to civil claims and criminal prosecutions.

Despite all the greed and corruption, Gordhan is optimistic about where the country is headed, but he knows it's going to be a tough road to achieve the vision of the Freedom Charter.

◈

Sandy Africa, who met Gordhan in the 1980s when he was already regarded as a 'very senior and authoritative figure' in the struggle, peppers our conversation about Gordhan with the description of him being 'principled'. But, she adds, 'perhaps on a more academic level, a question that I sometimes interrogate is whether the ANC's adoption of neoliberal policies and, by implication, his engagements with the business community and just how politics is playing out, is not a kind of a path to an inevitably failed or flawed or poorer outcome.'

There are, of course, many nuances and different varieties, but 'neoliberal' has broadly come to mean policies that promote free-market capitalism or, as the Cambridge Dictionary puts it, rather pithily, 'supporting a large amount of freedom for markets, with little government control or spending, and low taxes'.

'Neoliberal' isn't a word that rolls easily off Gordhan's tongue. He tells of how a friend showed him a Facebook comment 'from some-body who said I must change my neoliberal views'. 'Now, clearly the guy doesn't know me or doesn't understand my politics or has ever heard me speak publicly,' he says with an exasperated laugh.

As mentioned, Gordhan believes the mainstream business com-munity and the country's 'commentariat' are set in a 'very conservative neoliberal' mould and see the world from this perspective in spite of it having moved on, particularly since the Covid-19 pandemic laid bare the downside of such a system.

So Gordhan is definitely not a neoliberal. But what is he?

Gordhan keeps returning to the aspirations of the Freedom Charter, whose ideals shaped him as a young activist and whose prin-ciples were his guiding lights. It's evident that he remains committed to its sentiments, particularly the clause that 'South Africa belongs to all who live in it'. Many stress that he sees the upliftment of the poor as a key to the country's future.

He also quite often talks about himself as being a 'Congressite' – an advocate of the Congress Alliance, which included the ANC.

Friends say he is indeed a Congressite, to his core. One says, 'He lives the central values espoused by Congress – non-racialism, non-sexism and a united South Africa with an abiding commitment to social justice. These values are inscribed in the constitution of a democratic South Africa, which he had such a powerful hand in negotiating.'

As finance minister, Gordhan had a hand on the tiller of the country's economy and he continues to influence it in the public enterprises portfolio. In this context, he appears to be an advocate of Mariana Mazzucato's thinking, where the state is the shaper of markets and contributes to the creation of public value.

Gordhan points out that thinkers from around the world are raising powerful questions about liberal democracy, the economic system, and how those things are in danger unless they begin to change, and to take account of what ordinary people need. 'So it's an exciting time to rethink many of the things that we thought we knew, and we understood, because the pandemic has provided us with a whole new set of challenges, whether it's climate change, looking after the environment, the issue of violence against women …'

He says the pandemic has exposed faultlines in societies. 'Ours has its own peculiar set of faultlines coming from its own history. There's the formal politics, there's the formal economy, and then there's the real life of people on the ground. And that's where I started forty-odd years ago. And then the question then was, "How do we mobilise and organise people in order to give them a greater control over their lives, but also [so they can] become participants in the process of producing a democracy?"

'I see around the world there are some interesting experiments. And there are some remarkable discoveries of people who provide leadership in their own little local context – we would have it in the form of stokvels, burial societies, welfare societies, informal networks, child-welfare organisations, etcetera. And how you empower those organisations to play both the specific role but also a wider role in the context of unemployment and more hope for young people –

a kind of passageway between despair and joblessness, on the one hand, and a purpose-driven life for young people that contributes to the national cause and their own development, [on the other] – is a kind of interesting challenge, I think, that we've got.'

He believes that 'the controllers of wealth in South Africa haven't really broken through the old moulds adequately yet'. They've realised there are new business opportunities 'on the other side, but not in terms of finding a new path where some sacrifices are made in order to become a lot more inclusive as far as the economy is concerned'. 'I've been talking about that for about ten years. Some get it now, but most don't get it .... that this is the long-term investment you need to make in this society. And then you'll have, in ten, fifteen years, a very different middle class.

'Optimism is certainly there, the vision of a different South Africa is certainly there, but we need more effort being put into creating a more fluid and collaborative climate between key sectors of power in society.'

⚜

Gordhan's mission as minister of public enterprises isn't over. Although the 72-year-old official knows he can't sit in a government position forever, he has no plans to retire just yet, and for the time being he's still firmly ensconced in his government seat. 'If my health keeps me going and if the president still needs me, I'll stick around for a while,' he says.

Abbreviations

ANC: African National Congress
AWB: Afrikaner Weerstandsbeweging
Codesa: Convention for a Democratic South Africa
CoGTA: cooperative governance and traditional affairs
COSAG: Concerned South Africans Group
Cosas: Congress of South African Students
Cosatu: Congress of South African Trade Unions
CRU: community research unit
DA: Democratic Alliance
EFF: Economic Freedom Fighters
FSCA: Financial Sector Conduct Authority
GDP: gross domestic product
IFP: Inkatha Freedom Party
MDM: Mass Democratic Movement
MK: Umkhonto we Sizwe
MP: member of parliament
MPNF: Multiparty Negotiating Forum
NEC: national executive committee
NGO: non-governmental organisation
NIC: Natal Indian Congress
NP: National Party
NPA: National Prosecuting Authority
OCMS: organisation, consciousness, mobilisation and struggle
PAC: Pan Africanist Congress

PIC: Public Investment Corporation
RET: radical economic transformation
SAA: South African Airways
SACP: South African Communist Party
SAIC: South African Indian Congress
SARS: South African Revenue Service
SASO: South African Student Organisation
SIU: Special Investigative Unit
SOE: state-owned enterprise
SRC: student representative council
SSA: State Security Agency
TIC: Transvaal Indian Congress
TRC: Truth and Reconciliation Commission
UDF: United Democratic Front
VAT: value-added tax
Wits: University of the Witwatersrand

Sources and references

Information in this book is based on interviews conducted between May 2020 and June 2021, in person, via Zoom, email or WhatsApp, or on the phone, with the following people: Pravin Gordhan, Vani Gordhan, Mcebisi Jonas, Abba Omar, Ivan Pillay, Yousuf Vawda, Sunny Singh, Goolam Aboobaker, Moe Shaik, Shamim Meer, Vidhu Vedalankar, Mac Maharaj, Judge Thumba Pillay, Mpho Scott, Ismail 'Momo' Momoniat, Mandla Nkomfe, Sandy Africa, Dr Ebrahim 'Baker' Aboobaker, Roelf Meyer, Peter Richer, Derek Hanekom, Johann van Loggerenberg, Mandla Nkomfe, Jonathan Rosenthal, Goolam Ballim, Ann Crotty, Judge Dennis Davis and Murray Michell, as well as senior sources at the treasury, government officials, and a number of former comrades, colleagues, friends and associates of Gordhan who spoke to us on condition of anonymity.

African National Congress. N.d. 'Minutes and Accords between the ANC and the National Party Government, May 1990-February 1991'. https://web.archive.org/web/20060924080916/http://www.anc.org.za/ancdocs/history/transition/minutes.html Accessed 16 June 2021.

AmaShabalala, M. 2021. 'Zuma said intelligence report used to sack Gordhan and Jonas "may not exist": intelligence watchdog', TimesLive, 21 April. https://www.timeslive.co.za/politics/2021-04-21-zuma-said-intelligence-report-used-to-sack-gordhan-and-jonas-may-not-exist-intelligence-watchdog/ Accessed 28 June 2021.

Bezuidenhout, J. 2018. 'Nene state capture testimony reveals web of deceit and lies wound around Treasury and officials', Daily Maverick, 3 October. https://www.dailymaverick.co.za/article/2018-10-03-nene-state-capture-testimony-reveals-web-of-deceit-and-lies-wound-around-treasury-and-officials/ Accessed 15 June 2021.

BizNews. 2016. 'Trevor Manuel joins other ANC stalwarts, wants oath-breaking Zuma to resign', 5 April. www.biznews.com/sarenewal/

2016/04/05/trevor-manuel-joins-other-anc-stalwarts-wants-oath-breaking-zuma-to-resign Accessed 15 June 2021.

Bloomberg. 2016. 'Apartheid steeled Gordhan for political warfare', Tech Central, 31 October. https://techcentral.co.za/apartheid-steeled-gordhan-for-political-warfare/69659/ Accessed 15 June 2021.

Chemaly, F. 2020. 'Tin Town: Before and after the flood', *Independent on Saturday*, 31 May. https://www.iol.co.za/ios/behindthenews/tin-town-before-and-after-the-flood-48709056 Accessed 16 June 2021.

Constitution Hill. N.d. The Archive of the Constitution-Making Process. https://ourconstitution.constitutionhill.org.za/south-african-constitution/archive/ Accessed 15 June 2021.

Corruption Watch. 2014. 'Local govt going back to basics,' 19 September. https://www.corruptionwatch.org.za/local-govt-going-back-to-basics/ Accessed 15 June 2021.

Corruption Watch. 2018. 'In the Judicial Commission of Inquiry into Allegations of State Capture, Corruption and Fraud in the public sector including organs of state: Statement by Pravin Jamnadas Gordhan regarding terms of reference 1.1 to 1.3', 11 October. www.corruptionwatch.org.za/wp-content/uploads/2018/11/Pravin-Gordhan-Zondo-statement.pdf Accessed 15 June 2021.

Cowan, K, Masondo, S and Karrim, A. 2021. 'The Eskom Files: Power utility's R178 000 000 000 dodgy tender tsunami', *News24*, 3 May. https://www.news24.com/news24/southafrica/investigations/eskomfiles/the-eskom-files-exclusive-power-utilitys-r178-000-000-000-dodgy-tender-tsunami-20210503 Accessed 15 June 2021.

Cronje, J and Smith, C. 2019. 'Financial regulator raids office of Iqbal Survé', *Fin24*, 9 October. https://www.news24.com/fin24/Companies/Investment-Holdings/financial-regulator-raids-offices-of-iqbal-surve-20191009 Accessed 15 June 2021.

Dasnois, A and Whitfield, C. 2019. *Paper Tiger: Iqbal Survé and the Downfall of Independent Newspapers*. Tafelberg.

Defense Advanced Research Projects Agency (Darpa). N.d. https://www.darpa.mil/ Accessed 15 June 2021.

Desai, A. 2020. 'Slurs, slander and slang: The red overalls' racist insults need to be called out for what they are', *Daily Maverick*, 7 February. https://www.dailymaverick.co.za/opinionista/2020-02-27-slurs-slander-and-slang-the-red-overalls-racist-insults-need-to-be-called-out-for-what-they-are/ Accessed 15 June 2021.

Dlamini, S and Mdluli, A. 2019. 'Union slams FSCA raid on Iqbal Survé businesses', IOL, 13 October. https://www.iol.co.za/news/politics/union-slams-fsca-raid-on-iqbal-surve-businesses-34817434 Accessed 15 June 2021.

Dludla, N. 2021. 'South African government sells majority stake in SAA to consortium', Reuters, 11 June. https://www.reuters.com/business/ aerospace-defense/consortium-take-51-stake-south-african-airways- minister Accessed 24 June 2021.

eNCA. 2017. 'The rise and decline of outgoing ANC leader Jacob Zuma', 18 December. https://www.enca.com/south-africa/profile-anc-president- jacob-zuma Accessed 15 June 2021.

Freedom Charter. 1955. https://scnc.ukzn.ac.za/doc/hist/freedomchart/ freedomch.html Accessed 15 June 2021.

Gasa, N. 2018. '"Indian cabal" narrative is to protect the looting project', *City Press*, 19 November. https://www.news24.com/citypress/voices/ indian-cabal-narrative-is-to-protect-the-looting-project-20181119 Accessed 15 June 2021.

Gebrekidan, S and Onishi, N. 2018. 'Corruption gutted South Africa's tax agency. Now the nation is paying the price', *The New York Times*, 10 June. https://www.nytimes.com/2018/06/10/world/africa/south-africa-corruption- taxes.html Accessed 15 June 2021.

Govender, N and Chetty, V. 2014. *Legends of the Tide: Roots of the Durban Fishing Industry*. Rebel Rabble.

GroundUp. 2017. 'Huge crowd cheers Pravin Gordhan at St Georges Cathedral', 6 April. https://www.groundup.org.za/article/huge-crowd-cheers-pravin- gordhan-st-georges-cathedral/ Accessed 15 June 2021.

Harber, A. 2020. *So, For The Record: Behind the Headlines in an Era of State Capture*. Jonathan Ball Publishers.

Hood, T. 2020. 'The "Jamnandas" issue: Malema denies racially abusing Pravin Gordhan', *The South African*, 28 February. https:// www.thesouthafrican.com/news/eff-eskom-march-julius-malema-what-does- jamnandas-mean-why-is-it-racist/ Accessed 24 June 2021.

Innovations for Successful Societies. N.d. 'Reworking the Revenue Service: Tax Collection in South Africa, 1999-2009'. Princeton University https://successfulsocieties.princeton.edu/sites/successfulsocieties/files/ South%20Africa%20SARS_1.pdf Accessed 15 June 2021.

Innovations for Successful Societies. 2010. Pravin Gordhan interviewed by David Hausman, 26 February. Princeton University's Oral History program, https://successfulsocieties.princeton.edu/sites/successfulsocieties/files/R4_CS_ DH_Gordhan_Cleared_RJ_v1.pdf Accessed 15 June 2021.

IOL. 2021. 'ANA is not a front for the SSA and won't be drawn into factional wars', 26 January. https://www.iol.co.za/news/politics/ ana-is-not-a-front-for-the-ssa-and-wont-be-drawn-into-factional-wars- 9e0f4087-3e77-4992-82fa-bae53dc27883. Accessed 15 June 2021.

IOL. 2021. 'We're keeping score! Our performance report of President Rama- phosa and his Cabinet', 7 January. https://www.iol.co.za/dailynews/news/ were-keeping-score-our-performance-report-of-president-ramaphosa-and-his-cabinet-b70bcd57-9f35-4477-9eb0-66975f025f1d Accessed 15 June 2021.

Kajee, A. 2107. 'Even if Zuma goes, South Africa will remain divided', Al Jazeera, 3 April. https://www.aljazeera.com/opinions/2017/4/3/even-if-zuma-goes-south-africa-will-remain-divided Accessed 15 June 2021.

Karrim, A. 2019. '"Mr Bongo must stop hallucinating" - Poisoning claims are nonsensical and outrageous, says Gordhan's spokesperson', *News24*, 22 November. https://www.news24.com/news24/southafrica/news/mr-bongo-must-stop-hallucinating-poisoning-claims-against-gordhan-are-nonsensical-and-outrageous-20191122 Accessed 15 June 2021.

Le Roux, J, Cowan, K, Du Toit, P and Basson, A. 2018. 'Fact checked: EFF's charges against Pravin Gordhan', News24, 28 November. https://www.news24.com/news24/Analysis/fact-checked-julius-malemas-charges-against-pravin-gordhan-20181128 Accessed 15 June 2021.

Maeko, T and Omarjee, H. 2021. 'Gordhan unveils sale of 51% stake in SAA', *Business Day*, 11 June. https://www.businesslive.co.za/bd/national/2021-06-11-gordhan-confirms-that-51percent-of-saa-will-be-sold/ Accessed 24 June 2021.

Mazzucato, M, Qobo, M and Kattel, R. 2021. 'Building state capacities and dynamic capabilities to drive social and economic development: The case of South Africa'. UCL Institute for Innovation and Public Purpose. https://www.ucl.ac.uk/bartlett/public-purpose/sites/public-purpose/files/final_the_case_of_south_africa_mazzucato_kattel_qobo_21-09.pdf Accessed 15 June 2021.

Meer, I. 2002. *A Fortunate Man*, Zebra Press.

Muller, A. 2017. 'Gordhan echoes ANC's socialist values at Kathrada's Cape Town memorial', *Daily Maverick*, 7 April. https://www.dailymaverick.co.za/article/2017-04-07-gordhan-echoes-ancs-socialist-values-at-kathradas-cape-town-memorial/ Accessed 15 June 2021.

Naidoo, S. 2019. 'This month marks 70 years since the horrific 1949 race riots', *The Post*, 13 January. https://www.iol.co.za/thepost/this-month-marks-70-years-since-the-horrific-1949-race-riots-18783849 Accessed 15 June 2021.

Nelson Mandela Foundation. 1993. Televised address to the nation by ANC President, Nelson Rolihlahla Mandela, on the assassination of Chris Hani, 13 April. http://db.nelsonmandela.org/speeches/pub_view.asp?pg=item&ItemID=NMS135&txtstr=Chris%20Hani Accessed 16 June 2021.

News24. 2018. 'Read Standard Bank's full statement to Zondo commission', 17 September. https://www.news24.com/news24/Columnists/GuestColumn/read-standard-banks-sintons-full-statement-to-zondo-commission-20180917 Accessed 15 June 2021.

News24. 2019. 'Rand was much weaker year after Nenegate, Treasury economist tells #Statecaptureinquiry', 19 February. https://www.news24.com/news24/SouthAfrica/News/live-more-treasury-witnesses-to-take-the-stand-as-state-capture-continues-20190219 Accessed 15 June 2021.

Norbrook, N. 2010. 'Portrait: Pravin Gordhan, SA finance minister', *The Africa Report*, 19 October. https://www.theafricareport.com/8978/ portrait-pravin-gordhan-sa-finance-minister/ Accessed 15 June 2021.

O'Malley: The Heart of Hope. N.d. 'The National Peace Accord and Its Structures'. https://omalley.nelsonmandela.org/omalley/index.php/site/q/03lv02424/04lv03275/05lv03294/06lv03321.htm Accessed 16 June 2021.

O'Malley: The Heart of Hope. 2003. '30 Jan 2003: Gordhan, Pravin' https://omalley.nelsonmandela.org/omalley/index.php/site/q/03lv03445/04lv03833/05lv03891/06lv03898.htm Accessed 22 June 2021.

O'Malley: The Heart of Hope. 2003. '19 Jun 2003: Nair, Billy' https://omalley.nelsonmandela.org/omalley/index.php/site/q/03lv00017/04lv00344/05lv01435/06lv01449.htm Accessed 22 June 2021.

O'Malley: The Heart of Hope. N.d. 'The death of Chris Hani – an African misadventure' by Arthur Kemp. https://omalley.nelsonmandela.org/ omalley/index.php/site/q/03lv02424/04lv03370/05lv03422.htm Accessed 15 June 2021.

O'Malley: The Heart of Hope. 1990. 'Report of the Commission on the Cabal'. 14 March. https://omalley.nelsonmandela.org/omalley/index.php/ site/q/03lv03445/04lv04015/05lv04154/06lv04181.htm Accessed 15 June 2021.

O'Malley: The Heart of Hope. 1998. '25 Aug 1998: Gordhan, Pravin' https:// omalley.nelsonmandela.org/omalley/index.php/site/q/03lv00017/04lv00344/ 05lv01183/06lv01236.htm Accessed 15 June 2021.

Onishi, N. 2015. 'Jacob Zuma appoints third finance minister of South Africa in a week', *The New York Times*, 14 December. https://www.nytimes. com/2015/12/15/world/africa/david-van-rooyen-south-africa-finance-minister-pravin-gordhan.html Accessed 15 June 2021.

Parkinson, J. 2017. 'South Africa party clash plays out at revered activist's funeral', *The Wall Street Journal*, 29 March. https://www.wsj.com/ articles/south-africa-party-clash-plays-out-at-revered-activists-funeral-1490807946 Accessed 15 June 2021.

Paton, C. 2021. 'A sparkling new moment of opportunity', *Business Day*, 14 June. https://www.businesslive.co.za/bd/opinion/columnists/ 2021-06-14-carol-paton-a-sparkling-new-moment-of-opportunity/ Accessed 24 June 2021.

Pauw, J. 2017. *The President's Keepers: Those Keeping Zuma in Power and out of Prison*. Tafelberg.

Pinnock, D. 1989. 'Culture and communication: The rise of the left-wing press in South Africa', *Race and Class*, https://core.ac.uk/download/pdf/8766806. pdf Accessed 15 June 2021.

Polity. 2019. Submissions by Minister Pravin Gordhan to the Zondo Commission of Inquiry, 13 March. https://www.polity.org.za/article/ submissions-by-minister-pravin-gordhan-to-the-zondo-commission-of-inquiry-2019-03-13 Accessed 15 June 2021.

Poplak, R. 2017. 'Trainspotter: The Long Goodbye – Gordhan and the anti-Zuma resistance hack the Kathrada memorial', *Daily Maverick*, 1 April. https://www.dailymaverick.co.za/article/2017-04-01-trainspotter-the-long-goodbyegordhan-and-the-anti-zuma-resistance-hack-the-kathrada-memorial/ Accessed 15 June 2021.

Powell, A. 2017. 'South Africa's embattled Zuma fires ministers who challenged him', VOA, 31 March. https://www.voanews.com/africa/south-africas-embattled-zuma-fires-ministers-who-challenged-him Accessed 15 June 2021.

Rabkin, F. 2019. 'ANC vet: Cabal report is a "distortion of reality"', *Mail & Guardian*, 2 October. https://mg.co.za/article/2019-10-02-anc-vet-cabal-report-is-a-distortion-of-reality/ Accessed 15 June 2021.

Rampedi, P, Dlamini, S and Mdluli, A. 2019. 'Watch as FSCA raids Iqbal Survé's offices in a "fishing expedition"', *Business Report*, 9 October. https://www.iol.co.za/business-report/companies/just-in-watch-as-fsca-raids-iqbal-surves-offices-in-a-fishing-expedition-34452193 Accessed 15 June 2021.

SABC News. 2018. 'State Capture Inquiry - Barbara Hogan, PT1', 12 November. YouTube, https://www.youtube.com/watch?v=oaq8CCo91yI Accessed 15 June 2021.

Saspu National. 1982. 'Campaign grows to get ex-detainee's job back', October. https://www.sahistory.org.za/sites/default/files/archive-files4/SNOct82.pdf Accessed 15 June 2021.

Seepe. S. 2020. 'Zondo Commission exposed Gordhan as petty, jealous, racist and dangerous', *The Star*, 3 December. https://www.iol.co.za/the-star/opin-ion-analysis/zondo-commission-exposed-gordhan-as-petty-jealous-racist-and-dangerous-65094c0f-6946-425a-894e-c35545a6c013 Accessed 15 June 2021.

Shaik, M. 2020. *The ANC Spy Bible: Surviving Across Enemy Lines.* Tafelberg.

Shange, N. 2018. 'Gordhan throws counter-punch, says EFF charges are based on lies', *TimesLive*, 27 November. https://www.timeslive.co.za/politics/2018-11-27-gordhan-throws-counter-punch-says-eff-charges-are-based-on-lies/ Accessed 15 June 2021.

Shivambu, F. 2018. 'Dismantling the Pravin Gordhan Cabal', 19 October. IOL, https://www.iol.co.za/news/opinion/dismantling-the-pravin-gordhan-cabal-17559524 Accessed 15 June 2021.

Sibanda, O. 2020. 'High court ruling on Mkhwebane's "rogue unit" report should throw legal profession into a tailspin', *Daily Maverick*, 8 December. https://www.dailymaverick.co.za/opinionista/2020-12-08-high-court-ruling-on-mkhwebanes-rogue-unit-report-should-throw-legal-profession-into-a-tail-spin/ Accessed 24 June 2021.

Sisulu, W. 1976. 'We Shall Overcome', The O'Malley archives, https://omalley.nelsonmandela.org/omalley/index.php/site/q/03lv01538/04lv02009/05lv02010/06lv02016/07lv02017.htm Accessed 25 June 2021.

Snyckers, T. 2020. 'The rogue unit that never was', *Financial Mail*,
8 December. https://www.businesslive.co.za/fm/opinion/2020-12-08-
telita-snyckers-the-rogue-unit-that-never-was/ Accessed 15 June 2021.

South African Government. 'Public Enterprises warns of fake news from
Sunday Independent', 7 March. https://www.gov.za/speeches/
cautionary-note-all-media-sunday-independent-7-mar-2020-0000
Accessed 15 June 2021.

South African History. 2019. 'Who is Ivan Pillay?' 30 May. Facebook, https://
www.facebook.com/SA.History/posts/who-is-ivan-
pillay-political-biographyborn-visvanathan-pillay-on-18-april-1953
-i/1950886198354416/ Accessed 15 June 2021.

South African History Online. N.d. '70. The Durban riots, 1949'. https://www.
sahistory.org.za/archive/70-durban-riots-1949 Accessed
15 June 2021.

South African History Online. N.d. 'Class, consciousness and organisation:
Indian political resistance in Durban, South Africa 1979-1996'
by Kumi Naidoo'. https://www.sahistory.org.za/archive/class-
consciousness-and-organisation-indian-political-resistance-durban-south-
africa-1979 Accessed 15 June 2021.

South African History Online. N.d. 'Jacob Gedleyihlekisa Zuma'. www.sahistory.
org.za/people/jacob-gedleyihlekisa-zuma Accessed 15 June 2021.

South African History Online. N.d. 'Negotiations and the transition'. https://
www.sahistory.org.za/article/negotiations-and-transition
Accessed 15 June 2021.

South African History Online. 2011. 'The Convention for a Democratic South
Africa'. 21 March. https://www.sahistory.org.za/article/convention-
democratic-south-africa-codesa-codesa-1 Accessed 16 June 2021.

Southern African Legal Information Institute. 2020. 'Gordhan and Others v
Public Protector and Others (36099/2098) [2020] ZAGPPHC 777,
17 December. http://www.saflii.org/za/cases/ZAGPPHC/2020/777.html
Accessed 15 June 2021.

Spector, B. 2013. 'The UDF at 30: An organisation that shook Apartheid's
foundation', *Daily Maverick*, 22 August. https://www.dailymaverick.co.za/
article/2013-08-22-the-udf-at-30-an-organisation-that-shook-apartheids-
foundation/ Accessed 20 July 2021.

State Capacity Research Project. 2017. 'Betrayal of the promise: How South
Africa is being stolen'. Public Affairs Research Institute, https://pari.org.za/
betrayal-promise-report/ Accessed 15 June 2021.

Statement on Inaugural Meeting of Presidential State-Owned Enterprises
Council. 2020. The Presidency, Republic of South Africa, 5 November. http://
www.thepresidency.gov.za/press-statements/statement-inaugural-
meeting-presidential-state-owned-enterprises-council
Accessed 15 June 2021.

Steytler, N and Powell, D. 2010. 'The impact of the global financial crisis on decentralized government in South Africa', *L'Europe en Formation*, 4:358. https://www.cairn.info/revue-l-europe-en-formation-2010-4-page-149.htm Accessed 15 June 2021.

Thamm, M. 2015. 'SARS rogue unit controversy: Investigative journalist claims Sunday Times was part of an "orchestrated effort"', *Daily Maverick*, 3 December. https://www.dailymaverick.co.za/article/2015-12-02-sars-rogue-unit-controversy-investigative-journalist-claims-sunday-times-was-part-of-an-orchestrated-effort/ Accessed 15 June 2021.

The Star. 2021. 'Gordhan's tactics at Zondo Commission shows he accounts to no one but himself', 25 March. https://www.iol.co.za/the-star/news/gordhans-tactics-at-zondo-commission-shows-he-accounts-to-no-one-but-himself-6acc1fc7-4d8c-42ac-9d59-d1570eaca7e3 Accessed 15 June 2021.

TimesLive. 2019. 'Read President Cyril Ramaphosa's state of the nation address', 7 February, https://www.timeslive.co.za/politics/2019-02-07-in-full-read-president-cyril-ramaphosas-state-of-the-nation-address/ Accessed 15 June 2021.

Truth and Reconciliation Commission of South Africa Final Report https://www.justice.gov.za/trc/report/

Truth and Reconciliation Commission Amnesty Committee - transcript of applications for amnesty by M Greyling, K Durr and FS Bothma in connection with the assault ('torture') of Messrs Pravin Gordhan and Raymond Lalla at or near Bethlehem in the Free State, https://www.justice.gov.za/trc/amntrans/1999/9908100903_dbn_990830dn.htm Accessed 16 June 2021.

Truth and Reconciliation Commission transcript, HJP Botha amnesty hearing, 19 and 20 August 1999, Durban. https://www.justice.gov.za/trc/amntrans/1999/9908100903_dbn_990820db.htm Accessed 22 June 2021.

Truth and Reconciliation Commission transcript, Lawrence Gerald Wasserman amnesty hearing, 19 August 1999, Durban. https://www.justice.gov.za/trc/amntrans/1999/9908100903_dbn_990819db.htm Accessed 22 June 2021.

Uncensored. 2018. '#SAPressFreedomDay: Piet Rampedi's Resignation Letter From Sunday Times', 19 October. https://uncensoredopinion.co.za/sapress-freedomday-piet-rampedis-resignation-letter-from-sunday-times/ Accessed 15 June 2021.

Van Loggerenberg, J. 2106. *Rogue: The Inside Story of SARS's Elite Crime-Busting Unit*. Jonathan Ball Publishers.

Vasagar, J. 2005. 'Mbeki fires deputy in corruption scandal', *The Guardian*, 15 June. https://www.theguardian.com/world/2005/jun/15/southafrica.jeevanvasagar Accessed 15 June 2021.

YouTube. 2018. 'Questions over SARS rogue unit from Pete Richer to Stephan Hofstatter', 21 September. https://www.youtube.com/watch?v=ds788N4U5-4 Accessed 15 June 2021.

Acknowledgements

We're indebted to Jeremy Boraine, Caren van Houwelingen and the team at Jonathan Ball Publishers for their commitment and support during this project. We're also grateful to Tracey Hawthorne, who, with her razor-sharp editor's knife, helped us shape the manuscript.

We would like to thank the people who shared their experiences and entrusted us with their memories – especially the 'unsung' Durban activists from the 1970s. A special note of thanks (and an apology) to Nthabiseng Borotho and Busisiwe Sokhulu: thank you for doing the impossible and finding time for us in Pravin Gordhan's hectic schedule and so sorry for all our nagging.

Finally, to Minister Gordhan: thank you for being so generous with your time and indulging all our questions.

> A huge thanks to my wife, Nicola, for giving the manuscript its first read and making many valuable suggestions. And the rest of our family – Kate, Kirsten, Robynne, James and Mia (a ray of sunshine when the world was suddenly plunged into gloom) – for their support.
>
> – *Chris Whitfield*

> To my family, Julian, Sterna, Judith, Andrew, Gabriel, Ruth, Mark, Zara, Alon, Charles, Romy, Daniel, Tali, the world-famous Gilad (Up The Bucs), Mom and Dad, thank you for all your love. To Sam and Kash (welcome to the

family), Khwezi, Rachel and Maya: you impress me all the time.

To Rachel's guardian angels: Dr Marc Hendricks, Terry Schlaphoff and Rachel's genetic twin, the amazing Magdalena Lewandowska – we will never have the words to say thank you, but we'll keep trying. (PS: anyone still reading this, please consider joining the SA Bone Marrow Registry, sabmr.co.za.)

And to Jean, without whom …

– Jonathan Ancer

Index

JONATHAN ANCER is an award-winning journalist who has worked as a reporter at *The Star*, a features writer for magazines, and a crossword columnist. This is his fourth book.

CHRIS WHITFIELD has been a journalist for forty years and is a former editor of the *Cape Times*, the *Cape Argus*, the *Weekend Argus* and acting editor of *The Witness* and the *Daily Sun*. Prior to becoming an editor he was a political correspondent for *The Star*. This is his third book.